Copycat Cookbook for Beginners

A Step-by-Step Manual for Aspiring Chefs, Delving into the World of Copycat Cooking, from Simple Staples to Gourmet Delights

by Ethan Leo

TABLE OF CONTENTS

INTRODUCTION

"Welcome to the flavorful realm of the 'Copycat Cookbook for Beginners'—your ultimate companion on a culinary journey that transcends the boundaries of ordinary home cooking. If you've ever found yourself savoring a restaurant dish and wondered, 'Can I make this at home?'—you're in the right place.

This cookbook is not just a collection of recipes; it's an invitation to delve into the art of copycat cooking, a craft that allows you to recreate the magic of your favorite restaurant meals right in your kitchen. Whether you're a novice chef taking your first steps into the culinary world or a seasoned cook seeking to expand your repertoire, this book is designed to inspire and guide you.

Unleashing Your Inner Chef

In the following pages, you'll embark on a culinary adventure that demystifies the secrets behind beloved dishes. We believe that everyone can be a chef, and copycat cooking provides a fun and accessible way to unleash your creativity in the kitchen. From the simplest staples to the most decadent gourmet creations, we've crafted recipes that cater to various tastes and skill levels.

A Step-by-Step Approach

Fear not if you're new to the kitchen—our step-by-step approach ensures you understand each technique and concept. We've carefully curated a diverse selection of recipes, ranging from familiar comfort foods to upscale delicacies, all presented in a format that makes them approachable and achievable.

Insider Insights and Time-Saving Tips

As you embark on your copycat cooking adventure, we share insider insights and time-saving tips to streamline your cooking process. Discover the subtle techniques that bring authenticity to your creations, allowing you to capture the essence of your favorite restaurant flavors without leaving your home.

Gourmet Dreams

For those who aspire to culinary greatness, our 'Copycat Cookbook for Beginners' is a gateway to gourmet dreams. Elevate your skills by tackling sophisticated recipes inspired by the finest dining experiences, and impress your guests with dishes that rival those of renowned establishments.

Prepare to transform your kitchen into a hub of culinary innovation, where the joy of copycat cooking becomes a delightful and rewarding part of your everyday life. So, grab your apron, sharpen those knives, and embark on a delicious journey together. The world of copycat cooking awaits, and we're thrilled to have you join us!"

HOMEMADE MCDONALD'S EGG MCMUFFIN

Cooking Time: 15 minutes
Serving: 1
Ingredients:

- 1 English muffin, split and toasted
- 1 large egg
- 1 slice of Canadian bacon
- 1 slice of American cheese
- Butter (for cooking)
- Salt and pepper to taste

Steps:

1. **Prepare the English Muffin:** Toast the English muffin halves until golden brown.

2. **Cook the Canadian Bacon:** In a skillet over medium heat, cook it until it's heated through and slightly crispy around the edges. Remove from the skillet and set aside.

3. **Fry the Egg:** Add a small amount of butter in the same skillet. Crack the egg into the skillet, season with salt and pepper, and cook to your desired doneness. For an authentic McMuffin experience, you may want a slightly runny yolk.

4. **Assemble the McMuffin:**

- Place the cooked egg on the bottom half of the toasted English muffin.
- Add the slice of Canadian bacon on top of the egg.
- Top with a slice of American cheese.
- Finally, place the other half of the toasted English muffin on top to create a sandwich.

1. **Serve:** Your Homemade McDonald's Egg McMuffin is ready to be enjoyed! Serve it warm.

Nutrition Facts: THESE VALUES ARE APPROXIMATE AND MAY VARY BASED ON SPECIFIC INGREDIENTS.

- Calories: 350
- Protein: 20g
- Carbohydrates: 30g
- Fat: 16g
- Saturated Fat: 7g
- Cholesterol: 220mg
- Sodium: 800mg
- Fiber: 2g
- Sugar: 2g

STARBUCKS INSPIRED SPINACH AND FETA WRAP

Cooking Time: 20 minutes
Serving: 2 wraps
Ingredients:

- 4 whole wheat tortillas

- 2 cups fresh spinach leaves, washed and dried
- 1 cup crumbled feta cheese
- 4 large eggs
- 1 tablespoon olive oil
- 1 teaspoon garlic powder
- Salt and pepper to taste
- Optional: 1/2 cup diced tomatoes for added freshness

Steps:

1. **Prepare the Spinach:** Heat olive oil over medium heat in a pan. Add fresh spinach and sauté until wilted, about 2-3 minutes. Season with garlic powder, salt, and pepper. Set aside.

2. **Scramble the Eggs:** In the same pan, scramble until fully cooked. Season with salt and pepper to taste.

3. **Assemble the Wrap:** Lay out each tortilla and divide the sautéed spinach evenly among them. Add scrambled eggs to the spinach, followed by crumbled feta cheese. If desired, sprinkle diced tomatoes over the filling.

4. **Fold the Wrap:** Fold in the sides of the tortilla and then roll it up tightly, creating a wrap.

5. **Heat the Wrap:** Place the wraps in a pan over medium heat and cook for 1-2 minutes on each side until the tortilla is golden brown and crispy.

6. **Serve:** Remove from heat and let them cool for a minute. Cut each wrap in half diagonally and serve.

Nutrition Facts (per wrap):

- Calories: 350
- Total Fat: 20g
    - Saturated Fat: 8g
    - Trans Fat: 0g
- Cholesterol: 230mg
- Sodium: 650mg
- Total Carbohydrates: 26g
    - Dietary Fiber: 4g
    - Sugars: 2g
- Protein: 18g

COPYCAT CRACKER BARREL PANCAKES

Cooking Time: 15 minutes
Servings: 4
Ingredients:

- 2 cups all-purpose flour
- 2 tablespoons granulated sugar
- 1 teaspoon baking soda
- 1 teaspoon baking powder
- 1/2 teaspoon salt
- 2 cups buttermilk
- 1/4 cup unsalted butter, melted

- 2 large eggs
- Cooking spray or additional butter for greasing the griddle

Steps:

1. Whisk together the flour, sugar, baking soda, baking powder, and salt in a large mixing bowl.

2. In a separate bowl, beat the eggs and add the buttermilk and melted butter. Mix well.

3. Pour the wet ingredients into the dry ingredients and stir until just combined. Be careful not to overmix; a few lumps are okay.

4. Preheat a griddle or a large non-stick skillet over medium heat. Lightly coat with cooking spray or butter.

5. Pour 1/4 cup portions of Batter onto the griddle for each pancake. Cook until bubbles form on the surface and the edges look set.

6. Flip the pancakes and cook the other side until golden brown. This should take about 2-3 minutes per side.

7. Remove the pancakes from the griddle and keep warm. Repeat until all the Batter is used.

Nutrition Facts (per serving):

- Calories: 350
- Total Fat: 12g
  - Saturated Fat: 7g
  - Trans Fat: 0g

- Cholesterol: 110mg
- Sodium: 700mg
- Total Carbohydrates: 48g
  - Dietary Fiber: 1g
  - Sugars: 10g
- Protein: 11g

DIY DUNKIN' DONUTS BLUEBERRY MUFFINS

Cooking Time: 25 minutes
Servings: 12 muffins
Ingredients:

- 2 cups all-purpose flour
- 1 cup granulated sugar
- 1 tablespoon baking powder
- 1/2 teaspoon baking soda
- 1/2 teaspoon salt
- 1 cup buttermilk
- 1/2 cup unsalted butter, melted
- 2 large eggs
- 1 teaspoon vanilla extract
- 1 1/2 cups fresh blueberries

Steps:

1. Preheat your oven to 375°F (190°C). Line a muffin tin with paper liners.

2. Whisk together the flour, sugar, baking powder, baking soda, and salt in a large bowl.

3. In a separate bowl, beat the buttermilk, melted butter, eggs, and vanilla extract until well combined.

4. Pour the wet ingredients into the dry ingredients and gently fold together until combined. Be careful not to overmix; a few lumps are okay.

5. Gently fold in the fresh blueberries until evenly distributed throughout the Batter.

6. Spoon the Batter into the prepared muffin tin, filling each cup about two-thirds full.

7. Bake in the preheated oven for 20-25 minutes or until a toothpick inserted into the center of a muffin comes out clean.

8. Allow the muffins to cool in the tin for 5 minutes, then transfer them to a wire rack to cool completely.

Nutrition Facts (per serving):

- Calories: 240
- Total Fat: 10g
    - Saturated Fat: 6g
    - Trans Fat: 0g
- Cholesterol: 55mg
- Sodium: 320mg
- Total Carbohydrates: 34g
    - Dietary Fiber: 1g

- Sugars: 17g
- Protein: 4g

INSPIRED CHICK-FIL-A CHICKEN BISCUIT

Cooking Time: 20 minutes
Serving: 4 biscuits
Ingredients:

- 4 boneless, skinless chicken breasts
- 1 cup buttermilk
- 1 cup all-purpose flour
- 1 cup seasoned breadcrumbs
- 1 teaspoon salt
- 1 teaspoon black pepper
- 1/2 teaspoon paprika
- 1/2 teaspoon garlic powder
- 1/2 teaspoon onion powder
- 1/4 teaspoon cayenne pepper (adjust to taste)
- 1 cup vegetable oil for frying
- 4 large biscuits, split and toasted
- Pickles, for serving

Steps:

1. **Marinate the Chicken:** In a bowl, combine the buttermilk, salt, black pepper, paprika, garlic powder, onion powder, and cayenne pepper. Place the chicken breasts in the mixture, ensuring

they are fully coated. Let it marinate in the refrigerator for at least 1 hour or overnight for the best flavor.

2. **Coat the Chicken:** Mix the flour and breadcrumbs in a shallow dish. Remove each chicken breast from the buttermilk marinade, allowing excess to drip off, and coat thoroughly with the flour mixture.

3. **Heat the Oil:** Heat the vegetable oil over medium-high heat until it reaches 350°F (180°C) in a large skillet.

4. **Fry the Chicken:** Carefully place the coated chicken breasts in the hot oil and fry for about 5-7 minutes per side until golden brown and cooked through. Ensure the internal temperature reaches 165°F (74°C).

5. **Assemble the Biscuits:** Toast the split biscuits. Place a fried chicken breast on the bottom half of each biscuit. Top with pickles and cover with the other half of the biscuit.

6. **Serve:** Serve the Inspired Chick-fil-A Chicken Biscuits warm. Optionally, serve with your favorite hot sauce or dipping sauce.

Nutrition Facts: (PER SERVING)

- Calories: 600
- Total Fat: 32g
    - Saturated Fat: 5g
    - Trans Fat: 0g

- Cholesterol: 80mg
- Sodium: 1200mg
- Total Carbohydrates: 45g
  - Dietary Fiber: 2g
  - Sugars: 3g
- Protein: 30g

PANERA BREAD'S CINNAMON CRUNCH BAGEL DELIGHT

Cooking Time: 20 minutes
Serving: 4 bagels
Ingredients:

- 4 plain bagels
- 1/2 cup unsalted butter, softened
- 1/2 cup brown sugar
- 1 teaspoon ground cinnamon
- 1 cup cinnamon crunch topping (store-bought or homemade)
- 4 ounces cream cheese, softened

Steps:

1. **Preheat Oven:** Preheat the oven to 350°F (175°C).
2. **Slice Bagels:** Slice the plain bagels in half and place them on a baking sheet.
3. **Cinnamon Sugar Butter Spread:** In a bowl, mix the softened butter, brown sugar, and ground

cinnamon until well combined. Spread this mixture generously on each bagel half.

4. **Apply Cinnamon Crunch Topping:** Sprinkle the cinnamon crunch topping evenly over the buttered bagel halves, pressing it gently so it adheres.

5. **Bake in the Oven:** Place the baking sheet in the oven and bake for about 12-15 minutes or until the edges are golden brown and the cinnamon crunch topping is crispy.

6. **Cool and Serve:** Remove the bagels from the oven and let them cool for a few minutes. Once cooled, spread softened cream cheese on each bagel half.

7. **Enjoy:** Serve these Panera Bread-inspired Cinnamon Crunch Bagels warm, and enjoy the delightful combination of sweet cinnamon, crunchy topping, and creamy cream cheese.

Nutrition Facts (per serving):

- Calories: 450
- Total Fat: 25g
    - Saturated Fat: 15g
    - Trans Fat: 0g
- Cholesterol: 65mg
- Sodium: 350mg
- Total Carbohydrates: 52g
    - Dietary Fiber: 2g
    - Sugars: 24g

- Protein: 7g

WAFFLE HOUSE HASH BROWNS AT HOME

Cooking Time: 20 minutes
Serving: 4
Ingredients:

- 4 large russet potatoes, peeled and grated
- 1/4 cup vegetable oil
- 1 teaspoon salt
- 1/2 teaspoon black pepper
- 1/2 teaspoon garlic powder
- 1/2 teaspoon onion powder
- 1/2 cup diced onions (optional)
- 1/2 cup shredded cheddar cheese (optional)
- Cooking spray

Steps:

1. **Preheat Waffle Iron:** Heat your waffle iron according to the manufacturer's instructions.

2. **Prepare Potatoes:** Using a clean kitchen towel or paper towels, squeeze out any excess moisture from the grated potatoes.

3. **Season Potatoes:** In a large bowl, combine the grated potatoes, salt, black pepper, garlic powder, and onion powder. Mix well to ensure even seasoning.

4. **Add Extras (Optional):** Mix in diced onions and shredded cheddar cheese for extra flavor if desired.

5. **Preheat Skillet:** Heat vegetable oil in a skillet over medium-high heat.

6. **Cook Potatoes in Skillet:** Add the seasoned potatoes to the skillet, spreading them out evenly once the oil is hot. Cook for 5-7 minutes or until the bottom is golden brown.

7. **Flip and Cook Again:** Flip the hash browns using a spatula and cook the other side until it's golden brown and the potatoes are cooked.

8. **Transfer to Waffle Iron:** Lightly coat the waffle iron with cooking spray. Transfer the partially cooked hash browns to the waffle iron, spreading them evenly.

9. **Cook in Waffle Iron:** Close the waffle iron and cook until the hash browns are crispy and golden brown on both sides.

10. **Serve:** Remove the hash browns from the waffle iron and serve hot. Garnish with additional salt and pepper if needed.

Nutrition Facts (per serving):

- Calories: 250
- Total Fat: 12g
  - Saturated Fat: 3g
  - Trans Fat: 0g
- Cholesterol: 10mg

- Sodium: 600mg
- Total Carbohydrates: 30g
  - Dietary Fiber: 3g
  - Sugars: 2g
- Protein: 5g

IHOP'S SIGNATURE STUFFED FRENCH TOAST

Cooking Time: 30 minutes

Servings: 4

Ingredients:

- 8 slices of thick-cut white bread
- 1 cup cream cheese, softened
- 1/2 cup strawberry preserves
- 4 large eggs
- 1 cup whole milk
- 1 teaspoon vanilla extract
- 1/2 teaspoon ground cinnamon
- 1/4 teaspoon salt
- 1/4 cup unsalted butter
- Powdered sugar for dusting
- Fresh strawberries for garnish

Steps:

1. **Prepare Filling:** Mix the softened cream cheese and strawberry preserves in a bowl until well combined.

2. **Make Sandwiches:** Spread the cream cheese mixture evenly on 4 slices of bread. Top each with another slice to make 4 sandwiches.

3. **Prepare Egg Mixture:** In a shallow dish, whisk together eggs, milk, vanilla extract, cinnamon, and salt.

4. **Dip and Coat:** Melt butter in a large skillet over medium heat. Dip each sandwich into the egg mixture, ensuring both sides are coated.

5. **Cook Sandwiches:** Place the coated sandwiches in the skillet and cook until golden brown on each side, about 3-4 minutes per side.

6. **Serve:** Remove from the skillet and let them cool slightly. Cut each sandwich diagonally and arrange it on plates. Dust with powdered sugar and garnish with fresh strawberries.

7. **Enjoy IHOP's Signature Stuffed French Toast!**

Nutrition Facts (per serving):

- Calories: 480
- Total Fat: 28g
  - Saturated Fat: 15g
  - Trans Fat: 0g
- Cholesterol: 230mg
- Sodium: 540mg

- Total Carbohydrates: 45g
  - Dietary Fiber: 2g
  - Sugars: 20g
- Protein: 12g

HEALTHY AVOCADO TOAST À LA FIRST WATCH

Cooking Time: 10 minutes
Serving: 2
Ingredients:

- 2 ripe avocados
- 4 slices whole-grain bread
- 1 tablespoon lemon juice
- Salt and pepper to taste
- 1 teaspoon red pepper flakes (optional)
- 4 poached eggs
- 1 tablespoon chopped fresh cilantro
- 1 teaspoon extra-virgin olive oil

Steps:

1. **Avocado Mash:** In a bowl, mash the ripe avocados with a fork until smooth. Add lemon juice, salt, and pepper to taste. Mix well.

2. **Toasting the Bread:** Toast the slices of whole-grain bread until golden and crispy.

3. **Assembly:** Spread the avocado mash evenly over each slice of toasted bread.

4. **Seasoning:** Sprinkle red pepper flakes on top for a hint of spice, if desired.

5. **Poached Eggs:** Prepare poached eggs to your liking. Place one poached egg on each slice of avocado-covered toast.

6. **Finishing Touches:** Drizzle a teaspoon of olive oil over the poached eggs. Garnish with chopped fresh cilantro.

7. **Serve:** Your Healthy Avocado Toast à la First Watch is ready to be served. Enjoy this nutritious and delicious breakfast!

Nutrition Facts (per serving):

- Calories: 320
- Total Fat: 20g
    - Saturated Fat: 3g
    - Trans Fat: 0g
- Cholesterol: 185mg
- Sodium: 320mg
- Total Carbohydrates: 28g
    - Dietary Fiber: 12g
    - Sugars: 3g
- Protein: 10g

CHEESY BACON GRITS ALA WAFFLE HOUSE

COOKING TIME:

- **Preparation Time:** 10 minutes

- **Cooking Time:** 30 minutes
- **Total Time:** 40 minutes

SERVINGS:

- **Yield:** 4 servings

INGREDIENTS:

- 1 cup stone-ground grits
- 4 cups water
- 1 teaspoon salt
- 1 cup shredded sharp cheddar cheese
- 1/2 cup grated Parmesan cheese
- 1/2 cup cooked and crumbled bacon
- 1/4 cup unsalted butter
- 1/2 teaspoon black pepper
- 1/4 cup heavy cream
- Chopped green onions for garnish

STEPS:

1. **Prepare Grits:**
   - In a medium saucepan, bring 4 cups of water to a boil. Stir in the grits and salt.
   - Reduce heat to low, cover, and simmer for 20-25 minutes or until the grits are thick and creamy, stirring occasionally.
2. **Add Cheeses and Bacon:**
   - Stir in the cheddar cheese, Parmesan cheese, and cooked bacon until the cheeses

are melted and the bacon is evenly distributed.

3. **Incorporate Butter and Cream:**
   - Add the butter, black pepper, and heavy cream to the grits. Stir until the butter is melted and the grits are smooth.

4. **Serve:**
   - Spoon the cheesy bacon grits into serving bowls.

5. **Garnish:**
   - Garnish with chopped green onions.

6. **Enjoy:**
   - Serve the Cheesy Bacon Grits hot and enjoy a delicious breakfast or brunch!

NUTRITION FACTS:

- **Serving Size:** 1 cup
- **Calories:** 400
- **Total Fat:** 28g
  - Saturated Fat: 16g
  - Trans Fat: 0g
- **Cholesterol:** 80mg
- **Sodium:** 800mg
- **Total Carbohydrates:** 25g
  - Dietary Fiber: 2g
  - Sugars: 0g
- **Protein:** 15g

DIY STARBUCKS SOUS VIDE EGG BITES

Cooking Time: 1 hour 30 minutes
Serving: 4
Ingredients:

- 4 large eggs
- 1/2 cup cottage cheese
- 1/4 cup grated Gruyere cheese
- 1/4 cup grated Monterey Jack cheese
- 1/4 cup spinach, chopped
- 1/4 cup red bell pepper, finely diced
- 1/4 cup cooked bacon, crumbled
- 1/2 teaspoon salt
- 1/4 teaspoon black pepper
- Cooking spray

Steps:

1. **Preheat Sous Vide:** Fill the sous vide precision cooker with water and set the temperature to 172°F (77.8°C).

2. **Prepare Egg Mixture:** In a blender, combine eggs, cottage cheese, Gruyere cheese, and Monterey Jack cheese. Blend until smooth.

3. **Add Mix-ins:** Stir in chopped spinach, diced red bell pepper, and crumbled bacon. Season with salt and pepper. Mix well.

4. **Prepare Jars:** Lightly coat four 8-ounce canning jars with cooking spray. Evenly distribute the egg mixture among the jars.

5. **Sous Vide Cooking:** Place the jars in the water bath, ensuring they are fully submerged. Cook for 1 hour.

6. **Remove and Cool:** Carefully remove the jars from the water bath using tongs. Allow the egg bites to cool for a few minutes.

7. **Serve:** Gently run a knife around the edge of each jar and invert the egg bites onto a plate. Serve warm.

Nutrition Facts (per serving):

- Calories: 220
- Total Fat: 15g
- Saturated Fat: 7g
- Cholesterol: 240mg
- Sodium: 590mg
- Total Carbohydrates: 3g
- Dietary Fiber: 1g
- Sugars: 1g
- Protein: 18g

INSPIRED BY DUNKIN' DONUTS OLD FASHIONED DONUTS

Cooking Time: 25 minutes
Serving: 12 donuts
Ingredients:

- 2 cups all-purpose flour

- 1 cup granulated sugar
- 1 teaspoon baking powder
- 1/2 teaspoon baking soda
- 1/2 teaspoon ground nutmeg
- 1/2 teaspoon salt
- 2/3 cup buttermilk
- 2 large eggs
- 1/4 cup unsalted butter, melted
- 1 teaspoon vanilla extract

For Glaze:

- 2 cups confectioners' sugar
- 1/4 cup milk
- 1 teaspoon vanilla extract

Steps:

1. Preheat your oven to 375°F (190°C) and grease a donut pan.
2. Whisk together the flour, sugar, baking powder, baking soda, nutmeg, and salt in a large bowl.
3. Whisk together the buttermilk, eggs, melted butter, and vanilla extract in another bowl.
4. Pour the wet ingredients into the dry ingredients and stir until just combined. Do not overmix.
5. Spoon the Batter into a piping or Ziploc bag with the corner cut off. Pipe the Batter into the prepared donut pan, filling each cavity about two-thirds full.

6. Bake for 12-15 minutes or until the edges are lightly golden. Allow the donuts to cool in the pan for 5 minutes before transferring them to a wire rack to cool completely.

For the Glaze:

1. Whisk together the confectioners' sugar, milk, and vanilla extract in a bowl until smooth.

2. Dip each cooled donut into the glaze, allowing any excess to drip off.

3. Place the glazed donuts back on the wire rack to set for about 15 minutes.

4. Serve and enjoy these inspired Dunkin' Donuts Old Fashioned Donuts with your favorite coffee!

Nutrition Facts (per serving):

- Calories: 240
- Total Fat: 5g
- Saturated Fat: 3g
- Cholesterol: 35mg
- Sodium: 180mg
- Total Carbohydrates: 45g
- Dietary Fiber: 1g
- Sugars: 28g
- Protein: 4g

HOMEMADE JAMBA JUICE ACAI BOWL

Cooking Time: 10 minutes

Serving: 2 bowls

Ingredients:

- 2 packs of frozen unsweetened acai berries
- 1 frozen banana
- 1/2 cup frozen mixed berries (strawberries, blueberries, raspberries)
- 1/2 cup almond milk (or any milk of your choice)
- 1 tablespoon honey or agave nectar
- 1/2 cup granola
- 1/4 cup shredded coconut
- Fresh fruits (such as sliced banana, berries, and kiwi) for topping
- Chia seeds for garnish

Steps:

1. **Prepare Acai Base:** Run the frozen acai berry packs under warm water for a few seconds to slightly thaw. Break them into chunks and place them in a blender.

2. **Blend Acai Base:** Add the frozen banana, mixed berries, almond milk, and honey/agave nectar to the blender. Blend until smooth and creamy.

3. **Assemble Bowls:** Divide the acai mixture between two bowls.

4. **Add Toppings:** Top each bowl with granola, shredded coconut, fresh fruits, and chia seeds.

5. **Serve:** Enjoy your Homemade Jamba Juice Acai Bowl immediately!

Nutrition Facts (per serving):

- Calories: 300
- Total Fat: 12g
  - Saturated Fat: 5g
  - Trans Fat: 0g
- Cholesterol: 0mg
- Sodium: 50mg
- Total Carbohydrates: 45g
  - Dietary Fiber: 8g
  - Sugars: 20g
- Protein: 5g
- Vitamin D: 2mcg
- Calcium: 150mg
- Iron: 2mg
- Potassium: 400mg

CRACKER BARREL'S SAWMILL GRAVY AND BISCUITS

Cooking Time: 20 minutes
Servings: 4
Ingredients:

- 2 cups whole milk
- 1/4 cup unsalted butter
- 1/4 cup all-purpose flour

- Salt and black pepper to taste
- 8 biscuits (store-bought or homemade)

Steps:

1. **Prepare Biscuits:** If using store-bought biscuits, bake them according to the instructions. If making homemade biscuits, follow your favorite recipe and have them ready.

2. **Make Roux:** In a skillet over medium heat, melt the butter. Once melted, add the flour and whisk continuously to form a roux. Cook for 2-3 minutes until the roux turns golden brown.

3. **Add Milk:** Gradually pour the whole milk, whisking constantly to avoid lumps. Continue whisking until the mixture thickens to your desired consistency.

4. **Season:** Season the gravy with salt and black pepper to taste. Keep in mind that the flavor will intensify as it simmers.

5. **Simmer:** Reduce the heat to low and let the gravy simmer for 5-7 minutes, allowing the flavors to meld. Stir occasionally.

6. **Serve:** Split the biscuits in half and place them on serving plates. Spoon the sawmill gravy generously over each biscuit.

7. **Garnish (Optional):** Garnish with additional black pepper or fresh herbs for added flavor and presentation.

Nutrition Facts (per serving):

- Calories: 350
- Total Fat: 18g
  - Saturated Fat: 10g
  - Trans Fat: 0g
- Cholesterol: 45mg
- Sodium: 400mg
- Total Carbohydrates: 40g
  - Dietary Fiber: 2g
  - Sugars: 6g
- Protein: 8g

COPYCAT TIM HORTONS BREAKFAST SANDWICH

Cooking Time: 15 minutes
Serving: 2 sandwiches
Ingredients:

- 4 English muffins, split and toasted
- 4 large eggs
- 4 slices Canadian bacon
- 4 slices cheddar cheese
- 2 tablespoons butter
- Salt and pepper to taste

Steps:

1. **Prepare Eggs:** In a non-stick skillet, melt 1 tablespoon of butter over medium heat. Crack the eggs into the pan and cook to your liking

(fried or scrambled). Season with salt and pepper.

2. **Cook Canadian Bacon:** In the same skillet, heat the Canadian bacon slices until they are warmed through and slightly crispy on the edges.

3. **Assemble Sandwiches:** On the bottom half of each toasted English muffin, place a slice of Canadian bacon, a cooked egg, and a slice of cheddar cheese. Top with the other half of the English muffin.

4. **Melt Cheese:** If the cheese hasn't melted completely, briefly place the sandwiches under the broiler until the cheese is gooey and bubbly.

5. **Serve:** Plate the sandwiches and serve them hot. Optionally, you can add your favorite hot sauce or ketchup.

Nutrition Facts (per serving):

- Calories: 450
- Total Fat: 25g
    - Saturated Fat: 12g
    - Trans Fat: 0.5g
- Cholesterol: 240mg
- Sodium: 800mg
- Total Carbohydrates: 30g
    - Dietary Fiber: 2g
    - Sugars: 2g
- Protein: 24g

MCDONALD'S HOTCAKES WITH SYRUP DUPLICATION

Cooking Time: 20 minutes
Serving: 4
Ingredients:

- 2 cups all-purpose flour
- 2 tablespoons sugar
- 1 tablespoon baking powder
- 1/2 teaspoon salt
- 1 1/2 cups milk
- 2 large eggs
- 1/4 cup unsalted butter, melted
- Cooking spray or additional butter for greasing the griddle
- Maple syrup for serving

Steps:

1. **Prepare the Dry Ingredients:** In a large mixing bowl, combine the flour, sugar, baking powder, and salt. Mix well to ensure an even distribution of ingredients.

2. **Mix the Wet Ingredients:** Whisk the milk and eggs in a separate bowl until well combined. Pour the melted butter into the mixture and whisk again until smooth.

3. **Combine Wet and Dry Mixtures:** Make a well in the center of the dry ingredients and pour the

wet ingredients into it. Stir gently until just combined. It's okay if there are a few lumps.

4. **Preheat the Griddle:** Preheat a griddle or a large non-stick skillet over medium heat. Lightly coat the surface with cooking spray or butter.

5. **Pour the Batter onto the Griddle:** Use a 1/4 cup measuring cup to pour the Batter onto the griddle, forming circles. Cook until bubbles form on the surface, then flip and cook the other side until golden brown.

6. **Repeat:** Continue this process until all the Batter is used, placing the cooked hotcakes on a plate and covering them with a kitchen towel to keep warm.

7. **Serve with Syrup:** Serve warm hotcakes drizzled with your favorite maple syrup.

Nutrition Facts (per serving):

- Calories: 380
- Total Fat: 14g
  - Saturated Fat: 8g
  - Trans Fat: 0g
- Cholesterol: 120mg
- Sodium: 580mg
- Total Carbohydrates: 52g
  - Dietary Fiber: 1g
  - Sugars: 12g
- Protein: 10g

STARBUCKS CARAMEL MACCHIATO CINNAMON ROLLS

Cooking Time: 2 hours (including rising time)
Servings: 12 rolls
Ingredients:

- For the Dough:
    - 1 cup warm milk (110°F/43°C)
    - 2 1/2 teaspoons active dry yeast
    - 1/2 cup granulated sugar
    - 1/3 cup unsalted butter, melted
    - 4 cups all-purpose flour
    - 1/2 teaspoon salt
    - 2 large eggs

- For the Filling:
    - 1/2 cup unsalted butter, softened
    - 1 cup brown sugar, packed
    - 2 tablespoons ground cinnamon
    - 1/2 cup finely chopped pecans (optional)

- For the Caramel Drizzle:
    - 1/2 cup caramel sauce (store-bought or homemade)
    - 1/4 cup heavy cream

Steps:

1. **Activate the Yeast:** Combine warm milk and yeast in a small bowl. Let it sit for 5 minutes until foamy.

2. **Prepare the Dough:** In a large mixing bowl, combine sugar, melted butter, flour, salt, and

eggs. Add the activated yeast mixture. Mix until a dough forms.

3. **Knead the Dough:** Turn the dough onto a floured surface and knead for 5-7 minutes until smooth. Place the dough in a greased bowl, cover with a damp cloth, and let it rise for 1 hour or until doubled in size.

4. **Roll Out the Dough:** Punch the risen dough into a 16x20-inch rectangle on a floured surface.

5. **Add the Filling:** Spread softened butter over the dough. Mix brown sugar and cinnamon and sprinkle it evenly. Add chopped pecans if desired.

6. **Roll and Cut:** Roll the dough tightly from the longer side. Cut into 12 even slices. Place in a greased baking dish.

7. **Rise Again:** Cover the rolls and let them rise for 30 minutes.

8. **Preheat and Bake:** Preheat the oven to 350°F (175°C). Bake the rolls for 25-30 minutes or until golden brown.

9. **Prepare the Caramel Drizzle:** Heat caramel sauce and heavy cream until well combined in a saucepan. Drizzle over warm cinnamon rolls.

10. **Serve and Enjoy:** Let the rolls cool for a few minutes before serving. Enjoy your Starbucks-inspired Caramel Macchiato Cinnamon Rolls!

Nutrition Facts (per serving): (NOTE: NUTRITIONAL VALUES MAY VARY BASED ON

SPECIFIC INGREDIENTS AND QUANTITIES USED)

- Calories: 350
- Total Fat: 15g
- Saturated Fat: 8g
- Cholesterol: 60mg
- Sodium: 180mg
- Total Carbohydrates: 50g
- Dietary Fiber: 2g
- Sugars: 25g
- Protein: 5g

WENDY'S INSPIRED BREAKFAST BUCCINATOR

Cooking Time: 20 minutes
Servings: 2
Ingredients:

- 4 slices of bacon
- 4 large eggs
- Salt and pepper, to taste
- 2 English muffins, split and toasted
- 2 slices of cheddar cheese
- 1 avocado, sliced
- Hot sauce (optional)

Steps:

1. **Cook Bacon:** In a large skillet over medium heat, cook the bacon until it reaches your desired level of crispiness. Remove the bacon from the skillet and set it on a paper towel-lined plate.

2. **Prepare Eggs:** In the same skillet, crack the eggs into the pan using the bacon fat. Season with salt and pepper. Cook the eggs to your liking (scrambled, over easy, or sunny-side up).

3. **Assemble English Muffins:** Place a slice of cheddar cheese on the bottom half of each toasted English muffin while cooking eggs. Place the English muffins on a baking sheet and broil in the oven for 1-2 minutes or until the cheese is melted.

4. **Assemble Buccinator:** Remove the English muffins from the oven once the cheese is melted. Top each muffin half with cooked bacon, a portion of the cooked eggs, and sliced avocado.

5. **Spice it Up (Optional):** Drizzle with hot sauce if you like a little heat.

6. **Complete the Buccinator:** Place the remaining halves of the English muffins on top to complete the Buccinator.

7. **Serve:** Serve the Wendy's Inspired Breakfast Buccinator immediately.

Nutrition Facts: (NOTE: NUTRITIONAL VALUES ARE APPROXIMATE AND MAY VARY BASED ON SPECIFIC INGREDIENTS AND SERVING SIZES.)

- Calories: 450 per serving
- Protein: 20g
- Fat: 30g
- Carbohydrates: 25g
- Fiber: 5g
- Sugar: 2g

PANERA BREAD'S MEDITERRANEAN VEGGIE BREAKFAST WRAP

Cooking Time: 20 minutes
Serving: 2 wraps
Ingredients:

- 4 large eggs
- Salt and pepper to taste
- 1 tablespoon olive oil
- 1/2 cup cherry tomatoes, halved
- 1/2 cup baby spinach leaves
- 1/4 cup crumbled feta cheese
- 1/4 cup diced red onion
- 2 whole wheat tortillas

Steps:

1. **Prepare the Eggs:** In a bowl, whisk the eggs and season with salt and pepper.

2. **Sauté Vegetables:** Heat olive oil in a skillet over medium heat. Add cherry tomatoes and cook

until slightly softened about 2 minutes. Add baby spinach and cook until wilted.

3. **Cook Eggs:** Push the vegetables to the side of the skillet and pour the whisked eggs into the empty space. Scramble the eggs until just set, then combine them with the vegetables.

4. **Assemble the Wrap:** Warm the whole wheat tortillas. Divide the egg and vegetable mixture between the two tortillas. Top with crumbled feta cheese and diced red onion.

5. **Wrap it Up:** Fold in the sides of the tortilla and then roll it up, creating a wrap.

6. **Serve:** Cut each wrap in half diagonally and serve immediately.

Nutrition Facts (per serving):

- Calories: 320
- Total Fat: 20g
    - Saturated Fat: 6g
    - Trans Fat: 0g
- Cholesterol: 380mg
- Sodium: 550mg
- Total Carbohydrates: 21g
    - Dietary Fiber: 4g
    - Sugars: 3g
- Protein: 15g

Healthy Copycat Smoothie King Smoothie
Cooking Time: 5 minutes

Serving: 2
Ingredients:

- 1 cup frozen mixed berries (strawberries, blueberries, raspberries)
- 1/2 banana, frozen
- 1/2 cup spinach leaves, fresh
- 1/2 cup kale leaves, fresh
- 1/4 cup Greek yogurt, plain
- 1 tablespoon chia seeds
- 1 tablespoon honey
- 1 cup almond milk, unsweetened
- Ice cubes (optional)

Steps:

1. **Prepare Ingredients:** Gather all the ingredients.
2. **Blend Greens:** In a blender, add the spinach and kale leaves.
3. **Add Fruits:** Add the frozen mixed berries and banana to the blender.
4. **Include Yogurt and Seeds:** Spoon Greek yogurt and add chia seeds.
5. **Sweeten with Honey:** Drizzle honey over the ingredients in the blender.
6. **Pour in Almond Milk:** Pour the unsweetened almond milk into the blender.
7. **Blend Until Smooth:** Blend all the ingredients until you achieve a smooth consistency. If the

smoothie is too thick, you can add more almond milk.

8. **Optional: Add Ice Cubes.** If you prefer a colder smoothie, add a handful of ice cubes and blend until smooth.

9. **Serve:** Pour the smoothie into glasses.

10. **Garnish (Optional):** Garnish with a few berries or a slice of banana for an extra touch.

Nutrition Facts (Per Serving):

- Calories: 180
- Protein: 7g
- Fat: 5g
- Carbohydrates: 30g
- Fiber: 8g
- Sugar: 18g
- Vitamin A: 50% Daily Value
- Vitamin C: 120% Daily Value
- Calcium: 20% Daily Value
- Iron: 6% Daily Value

OLIVE GARDEN'S ZUPPA TOSCANA SOUP

Cooking Time: 45 minutes

Servings: 6

Ingredients:

- 1 pound Italian sausage, casings removed
- 1 large onion, chopped
- 4 cloves garlic, minced
- 4 cups chicken broth
- 2 cups water
- 3 large potatoes, sliced into thin rounds
- 1 teaspoon red pepper flakes (adjust to taste)
- Salt and black pepper to taste
- 3 cups kale, chopped
- 1 cup heavy cream
- Grated Parmesan cheese for garnish

Steps:

1. In a large soup pot, brown the Italian sausage over medium heat, breaking it into small pieces with a spoon as it cooks. Once cooked, remove any excess fat.

2. Add the chopped onion to the pot and sauté until it becomes translucent.

3. Stir in the minced garlic and cook for an additional 1-2 minutes until fragrant.

4. Pour in the chicken broth and water, scraping the bottom of the pot to release any flavorful bits.

5. Add the sliced potatoes, red pepper flakes, salt, and black pepper. Bring the soup to a simmer and cook until the potatoes are tender (about 15-20 minutes).

6. Once the potatoes are cooked, add the chopped kale to the pot and cook for 3-5 minutes until the kale is wilted.

7. Pour in the heavy cream, stirring to combine. Let the soup simmer for 5-10 minutes to allow the flavors to meld.

8. Taste and adjust seasoning as needed. If you prefer a spicier soup, you can add more red pepper flakes at this point.

9. Serve the Zuppa Toscana hot, garnished with grated Parmesan cheese.

Nutrition Facts (per serving):

- Calories: 450
- Fat: 30g
- Saturated Fat: 12g
- Cholesterol: 75mg
- Sodium: 1200mg
- Potassium: 1200mg

- Carbohydrates: 30g
- Fiber: 3g
- Sugar: 3g
- Protein: 15g

CHIPOTLE-INSPIRED CHICKEN BURRITO BOWL

Cooking Time: 30 minutes

Serving: 4

Ingredients:

- 1 pound boneless, skinless chicken breasts, diced
- 1 tablespoon olive oil
- 1 teaspoon ground cumin
- 1 teaspoon chili powder
- 1/2 teaspoon garlic powder
- 1/2 teaspoon onion powder
- Salt and pepper to taste
- 1 cup cooked brown rice
- 1 can (15 ounces) black beans, drained and rinsed
- 1 cup corn kernels (fresh or frozen)
- 1 cup cherry tomatoes, halved
- 1 avocado, sliced
- 1/4 cup chopped fresh cilantro
- 1/2 cup shredded cheddar cheese
- 1/4 cup sour cream

- Lime wedges for garnish

Steps:

1. In a large skillet, heat olive oil over medium heat.

2. Add diced chicken to the skillet and season with cumin, chili powder, garlic powder, onion powder, salt, and pepper. Cook until the chicken is browned and cooked through.

3. In a separate pot, heat the black beans and corn over medium heat until warmed through.

4. Assemble the burrito bowls: Start with a base of brown rice, then top with seasoned chicken, black beans, corn, cherry tomatoes, avocado slices, cilantro, and shredded cheddar cheese.

5. Add a dollop of sour cream on top and garnish with lime wedges.

6. Serve immediately and enjoy your Chipotle-inspired chicken burrito bowl!

Nutrition Facts (per serving):

- Calories: 450
- Protein: 30g
- Carbohydrates: 40g
- Fiber: 10g
- Sugars: 3g
- Fat: 20g
- Saturated Fat: 6g
- Cholesterol: 80mg
- Sodium: 450mg

- Vitamin D: 5%
- Calcium: 20%
- Iron: 15%
- Potassium: 700mg

PANERA BREAD'S BROCCOLI CHEDDAR SOUP

Cooking Time: 30 minutes

Servings: 4

Ingredients:
- 1/4 cup unsalted butter
- 1/4 cup all-purpose flour
- 1/2 cup diced onion
- 1 cup julienned carrots
- 4 cups broccoli florets
- 4 cups low-sodium chicken broth
- 2 cups half-and-half
- 2 cups shredded sharp cheddar cheese
- Salt and pepper to taste
- 1/4 teaspoon nutmeg (optional)

Steps:
1. In a large pot, melt the butter over medium heat. Add diced onions and cook until softened.
2. Sprinkle flour over the onions and butter, stirring constantly to create a roux. Cook for 2-3 minutes

until the mixture thickens and becomes golden brown.

3. Slowly whisk in the chicken broth, ensuring no lumps form. Bring the mixture to a simmer.

4. Add julienned carrots and broccoli florets to the pot. Simmer for 15-20 minutes or until vegetables are tender.

5. Using an immersion blender, blend the soup until smooth, or transfer a portion to a blender and blend in batches.

6. Return the soup to low heat and add half-and-half, stirring continuously.

7. Gradually add shredded cheddar cheese, stirring until melted and well combined.

8. Season with salt, pepper, and nutmeg (if using). Adjust seasoning to taste.

9. Allow the soup to simmer for an additional 5 minutes to meld flavors.

10. Serve hot, garnished with additional shredded cheddar if desired.

Nutrition Facts (per serving):

- Calories: 450
- Total Fat: 35g
  - Saturated Fat: 21g
  - Trans Fat: 0g
- Cholesterol: 100mg
- Sodium: 800mg

- Total Carbohydrates: 20g
  - Dietary Fiber: 4g
  - Sugars: 5g
- Protein: 15g

HOMEMADE IN-N-OUT ANIMAL-STYLE BURGER

Cooking Time: 30 minutes

Serving: 4 burgers

Ingredients:

- 1 1/2 pounds ground beef (80% lean)
- Salt and pepper to taste
- 4 hamburger buns
- 4 slices American cheese
- 1/2 cup mayonnaise
- 2 tablespoons ketchup
- 1 tablespoon sweet pickle relish
- 1 teaspoon yellow mustard
- 1/2 cup finely chopped onions
- 1/4 cup dill pickles, chopped
- Vegetable oil for grilling
- Lettuce and tomato slices for topping

Steps:

1. **Preheat the grill:** Preheat your grill or stovetop pan over medium-high heat.

2. **Form the patties:** Divide the ground beef into 4 equal portions and shape them into patties. Season each patty with salt and pepper.

3. **Grill the patties:** Brush the grill with vegetable oil to prevent sticking. Grill the patties for about 3-4 minutes per side or until they reach your desired level of doneness. Place a slice of American cheese on each patty at the last minute of cooking.

4. **Prepare the sauce:** In a small bowl, mix together mayonnaise, ketchup, sweet pickle relish, and yellow mustard. Set aside.

5. **Toast the buns:** Cut the hamburger buns in half and toast them on the grill for about 1 minute or until golden brown.

6. **Assemble the burgers:** Spread a generous amount of the sauce on the bottom half of each bun. Place a cheese-covered patty on top. Sprinkle chopped onions and pickles over the patty. Add lettuce and tomato slices.

7. **Top it off:** Place the top half of the bun on the assembled burger.

8. **Serve:** Your Homemade In-N-Out Animal-Style Burgers are ready to be served! Enjoy them with your favorite side dishes.

Nutrition Facts (per serving):

- Calories: 650
- Total Fat: 45g
- Saturated Fat: 18g

- Cholesterol: 120mg
- Sodium: 980mg
- Total Carbohydrates: 28g
- Dietary Fiber: 2g
- Sugars: 7g
- Protein: 32g

CHILI'S COPYCAT SOUTHWESTERN EGG ROLLS

Cooking Time: 30 minutes

Servings: 4-6

Ingredients:

- 1 cup cooked and shredded chicken
- 1/2 cup black beans, drained and rinsed
- 1/2 cup corn kernels
- 1/4 cup diced red bell pepper
- 1/4 cup diced green onions
- 1/2 cup shredded Monterey Jack cheese
- 1 teaspoon ground cumin
- 1 teaspoon chili powder
- 1/2 teaspoon garlic powder
- Salt and pepper to taste
- 12 egg roll wrappers
- Vegetable oil for frying
- Sweet chili sauce for dipping

Steps:

1. Combine shredded chicken, black beans, corn, red bell pepper, green onions, Monterey Jack cheese, cumin, chili powder, garlic powder, salt, and pepper in a large bowl. Mix well.

2. Place an egg roll wrapper on a clean surface with one corner pointing towards you. Spoon about 2 tablespoons of the chicken mixture onto the center of the wrapper.

3. Fold the bottom corner over the filling, then fold in the sides and roll it up tightly. Use a small amount of water to seal the top corner. Repeat with the remaining wrappers.

4. In a deep skillet or fryer, heat vegetable oil to 350°F (175°C). Fry the egg rolls in batches until golden brown, about 2-3 minutes per batch. Remove with a slotted spoon and drain on paper towels.

5. Serve the Southwestern egg rolls warm with sweet chili sauce for dipping.

Nutrition Facts: *Note: Nutritional values are approximate and may vary based on specific ingredients.*

- Serving Size: 2 egg rolls
- Calories: 300
- Total Fat: 12g
- Saturated Fat: 4g
- Cholesterol: 35mg

- Sodium: 400mg
- Total Carbohydrates: 35g
- Dietary Fiber: 3g
- Sugars: 3g
- Protein: 15g

DIY SHAKE SHACK BURGER

Cooking Time: 20 minutes

Serving: 4 burgers

Ingredients:

- 1 pound ground beef (80% lean)
- 4 hamburger buns
- 4 slices of American cheese
- 1/2 cup mayonnaise
- 1 tablespoon ketchup
- 1 tablespoon yellow mustard
- 1 teaspoon pickle relish
- Salt and pepper to taste
- 4 leaves of fresh lettuce
- 1 large tomato, sliced
- 1/2 red onion, thinly sliced

Steps:

1. Preheat your grill or stovetop griddle over medium-high heat.

2. Divide the ground beef into 4 equal portions and shape them into patties. Season each patty with salt and pepper.

3. Place the patties on the grill or griddle and cook for 3-4 minutes per side for medium doneness.

4. In the last minute of cooking, place a slice of American cheese on each patty and cover with a lid to melt the cheese.

5. While the burgers are cooking, mix mayonnaise, ketchup, mustard, and pickle relish in a bowl to create a special sauce.

6. Toast the hamburger buns on the grill or in a toaster until lightly browned.

7. Assemble the burgers by spreading a generous amount of the special sauce on the bottom half of each bun.

8. Place a cooked patty with melted cheese on top of the sauce.

9. Add a leaf of lettuce, a couple of tomato slices, and a few slices of red onion.

10. Top with the other half of the bun and secure with a toothpick if needed.

Nutrition Facts: *(Per Serving)*

- Calories: 550
- Total Fat: 35g
    - Saturated Fat: 12g
    - Trans Fat: 1g
- Cholesterol: 95mg

- Sodium: 800mg
- Total Carbohydrates: 28g
  - Dietary Fiber: 2g
  - Sugars: 6g
- Protein: 30g

RED LOBSTER'S CHEDDAR BAY BISCUITS

Ingredients:
- 2 cups all-purpose flour
- 1 tablespoon sugar
- 1 tablespoon baking powder
- 2 teaspoons garlic powder
- 1/2 teaspoon salt
- 1/2 cup unsalted butter, cold and cut into small pieces
- 1 1/2 cups shredded sharp cheddar cheese
- 3/4 cup whole milk

Cooking Time: 15 minutes

Servings: 12 biscuits

Nutrition Facts (per serving):
- Calories: 220
- Total Fat: 15g
- Saturated Fat: 9g
- Cholesterol: 40mg

- Sodium: 350mg
- Total Carbohydrates: 17g
- Dietary Fiber: 0.5g
- Sugars: 1g
- Protein: 6g

Steps:

1. Preheat your oven to 450°F (230°C) and line a baking sheet with parchment paper.

2. Whisk together the flour, sugar, baking powder, garlic powder, and salt in a large mixing bowl.

3. Add the cold, cubed butter to the dry ingredients. Using a pastry cutter or your fingers, cut the butter into the flour mixture until it resembles coarse crumbs.

4. Stir in the shredded cheddar cheese until evenly distributed in the mixture.

5. Make a well in the center of the mixture and pour in the milk. Gently stir until just combined. Be careful not to overmix; the dough should be sticky.

6. Drop large spoonfuls of the dough onto the prepared baking sheet, spacing them about 2 inches apart.

7. Bake in the oven for 12-15 minutes or until the tops are golden brown.

8. While baking the biscuits, melt 2 tablespoons of butter and stir in 1/2 teaspoon of garlic powder.

Brush the garlic butter mixture over the tops once the biscuits are out of the oven.

9. Serve the Cheddar Bay Biscuits warm. They are best enjoyed fresh out of the oven.

INSPIRED STARBUCKS CHICKEN AND QUINOA PROTEIN BOWL

Cooking Time: 30 minutes

Servings: 2

Ingredients:

- 1 cup quinoa, rinsed
- 2 cups water
- 2 boneless, skinless chicken breasts
- 1 tablespoon olive oil
- Salt and pepper to taste
- 1 teaspoon paprika
- 1 teaspoon garlic powder
- 1 cup cherry tomatoes, halved
- 1 cucumber, diced
- 1/2 cup feta cheese, crumbled
- 1/4 cup red onion, finely chopped
- 1/4 cup Kalamata olives, sliced
- 2 cups baby spinach leaves

For the Dressing:

- 3 tablespoons balsamic vinegar

- 2 tablespoons extra-virgin olive oil
- 1 teaspoon Dijon mustard
- Salt and pepper to taste

Steps:

1. **Cook Quinoa:** In a medium saucepan, combine quinoa and water. Bring to a boil, then reduce heat to low, cover, and simmer for 15-20 minutes or until the quinoa is cooked and water is absorbed. Fluff with a fork and set aside.

2. **Prepare Chicken:** Season chicken breasts with salt, pepper, paprika, and garlic powder. In a skillet over medium heat, heat olive oil. Cook the chicken for 6-8 minutes per side or until cooked through. Remove from heat and let it rest for a few minutes before slicing.

3. **Make Dressing:** In a small bowl, whisk together balsamic vinegar, olive oil, Dijon mustard, salt, and pepper to create the dressing.

4. **Assemble Bowls:** In two serving bowls, divide the cooked quinoa. Top with sliced chicken, cherry tomatoes, cucumber, feta cheese, red onion, Kalamata olives, and baby spinach.

5. **Drizzle Dressing:** Pour the prepared dressing over the bowls.

6. **Toss and Serve:** Gently toss the ingredients in each bowl to combine flavors. Serve immediately.

Nutrition Facts (per serving):

- Calories: 480

- Protein: 30g
- Carbohydrates: 45g
- Fiber: 7g
- Sugar: 5g
- Fat: 20g
- Saturated Fat: 6g
- Cholesterol: 70mg
- Sodium: 600mg
- Vitamin D: 5%
- Calcium: 20%
- Iron: 25%
- Potassium: 900mg

CHEESECAKE FACTORY'S AVOCADO EGG ROLLS

Ingredients:
- 3 ripe avocados, peeled, pitted, and diced
- 1 cup sun-dried tomatoes, finely chopped
- 1/2 cup red onion, finely diced
- 1/4 cup fresh cilantro, chopped
- 1 tablespoon fresh lime juice
- Salt and pepper to taste
- 1 package egg roll wrappers
- Vegetable oil for frying

Cooking Time: 20 minutes

Serving: 4-6 people

Steps:

1. Combine the diced avocados, sun-dried tomatoes, red onion, cilantro, and lime juice in a large mixing bowl.

2. Season the mixture with salt and pepper to taste. Gently toss the ingredients until well combined.

3. Lay out an egg roll wrapper with one corner pointing towards you. Place a generous spoonful of the avocado mixture in the center of the wrapper.

4. Fold the bottom corner over the filling, then roll tightly in the sides. Use a small amount of water to seal the edge of the wrapper.

5. Heat vegetable oil in a deep fryer or a large, deep skillet to 350°F (175°C).

6. Carefully place the rolled egg rolls into the hot oil, a few at a time, and fry until golden brown, about 3-4 minutes. Use a slotted spoon to remove and drain on paper towels.

7. Repeat until all the egg rolls are cooked.

Nutrition Facts (per serving):

- Calories: 320
- Total Fat: 18g
    - Saturated Fat: 3g
    - Trans Fat: 0g
- Cholesterol: 0mg

- Sodium: 280mg
- Total Carbohydrates: 38g
  - Dietary Fiber: 7g
  - Sugars: 2g
- Protein: 5g

HOMEMADE PIZZA HUT SUPREME PERSONAL PAN PIZZA

Cooking Time: 25 minutes

Servings: 2 personal pan pizzas

Ingredients:

- 2 1/4 cups all-purpose flour
- 1 teaspoon sugar
- 1 teaspoon salt
- 1 tablespoon active dry yeast
- 1 cup warm water (110°F/43°C)
- 2 tablespoons olive oil

For the Pizza Toppings:

- 1/2 cup pizza sauce
- 1 cup shredded mozzarella cheese
- 1/2 cup sliced pepperoni
- 1/2 cup sliced bell peppers (mix of red and green)
- 1/2 cup sliced red onions
- 1/4 cup sliced black olives

- 1/4 cup sliced mushrooms

Steps:

1. **Prepare the Dough:**
   - Combine the warm water, sugar, and active dry yeast in a bowl. Let it sit for 5-10 minutes until it becomes frothy.
   - In a large mixing bowl, combine the flour and salt. Make a well in the center and pour the yeast mixture and olive oil. Mix until a dough forms.
   - Knead the dough on a floured surface for about 5 minutes until it becomes smooth and elastic.
   - Place the dough in a lightly oiled bowl, cover it with a damp cloth, and let it rise in a warm place for 1 hour or until it doubles in size.

1. **Preheat and Shape:**
   - Preheat the oven to 475°F (245°C).
   - Punch down the risen dough and divide it into two portions. Roll each portion into a 6-inch round.

1. **Assemble the Pizzas:**
   - Place the rounds on greased pizza pans or baking sheets.
   - Spread 1/4 cup of pizza sauce each round, leaving a small border around the edges.

- Sprinkle half of the shredded mozzarella cheese on each pizza.
- Add pepperoni, bell peppers, red onions, black olives, and mushrooms evenly.

1. **Bake:**

- Bake in the oven for 12-15 minutes or until the crust is golden and the cheese is bubbly and lightly browned.

1. **Serve:**

- Remove the pizzas from the oven and let them cool for a few minutes before slicing.
- Serve hot and enjoy your Homemade Pizza Hut Supreme Personal Pan Pizza!

Nutrition Facts (per serving): *Nutrition values are approximate and may vary based on specific ingredients used.*

- Calories: 650
- Total Fat: 24g
  - Saturated Fat: 9g
  - Trans Fat: 0g
- Cholesterol: 45mg
- Sodium: 1450mg
- Total Carbohydrates: 78g
  - Dietary Fiber: 5g
  - Sugars: 5g
- Protein: 28g

DIY SUBWAY CHICKEN TERIYAKI SANDWICH

Cooking Time: 25 minutes

Serving: 2 sandwiches

Ingredients:

- 2 boneless, skinless chicken breasts
- 1/2 cup teriyaki sauce
- 1 tablespoon vegetable oil
- 4 slices Swiss cheese
- 4 whole wheat sandwich rolls
- 1 cup shredded lettuce
- 1 tomato, sliced
- 1/2 red onion, thinly sliced
- 1/4 cup mayonnaise
- Salt and pepper to taste

Steps:

1. **Marinate Chicken:** Place chicken breasts in a zip-top bag and pour teriyaki sauce. Seal the bag and let it marinate in the refrigerator for at least 15 minutes.

2. **Cook Chicken:** Heat vegetable oil in a skillet over medium-high heat. Remove chicken from the marinade, season with salt and pepper, and cook for 6-8 minutes per side or until fully cooked. Ensure the internal temperature reaches 165°F (74°C). During the last minute of cooking, place a

slice of Swiss cheese on each chicken breast to melt.

3. **Prepare Rolls:** Cut the sandwich rolls in half while the chicken is cooking. Toast them in the oven or on a skillet until golden brown.

4. **Assemble Sandwiches:** Spread mayonnaise on the bottom half of each roll. Place a slice of Swiss cheese on the top half. Place the cooked chicken on the bottom half of the roll.

5. **Add Toppings:** Top the chicken with shredded lettuce, tomato slices, and red onion.

6. **Finish Assembling:** Place the top half of the roll with melted cheese over the toppings, creating a sandwich.

7. **Serve:** Cut each sandwich in half and serve immediately.

Nutrition Facts: *(Per Serving)*

- Calories: 550
- Total Fat: 22g
    - Saturated Fat: 7g
    - Trans Fat: 0g
- Cholesterol: 90mg
- Sodium: 1200mg
- Total Carbohydrates: 45g
    - Dietary Fiber: 6g
    - Sugars: 12g
- Protein: 40g

HOMEMADE PANDA EXPRESS ORANGE CHICKEN

Cooking Time: 40 minutes

Serving: 4

Ingredients:

- 1 lb boneless, skinless chicken thighs cut into bite-sized pieces
- 1 cup cornstarch
- 3 eggs, beaten
- 1/4 cup vegetable oil
- 1 cup orange juice
- 1/2 cup soy sauce
- 1/3 cup rice vinegar
- 1 cup brown sugar, packed
- 1/2 teaspoon ginger, minced
- 1/2 teaspoon garlic, minced
- 1/4 teaspoon red pepper flakes (adjust to taste)
- 2 tablespoons green onions, chopped (for garnish)
- Sesame seeds (for garnish)
- Cooked white rice (for serving)

Steps:

1. **Preparation:** In a large bowl, coat the chicken pieces in cornstarch, shaking off any excess. Dip each piece into beaten eggs, ensuring an even coating.

2. **Frying:** Heat vegetable oil in a large skillet over medium-high heat. Fry the coated chicken pieces until golden brown and crispy. Remove and place on a paper towel to absorb excess oil.

3. **Sauce:** In a separate saucepan, combine orange juice, soy sauce, rice vinegar, brown sugar, ginger, garlic, and red pepper flakes. Bring the mixture to a simmer over medium heat, stirring until the sugar dissolves. Allow it to simmer for 10-12 minutes or until the sauce thickens.

4. **Combine:** In a large bowl, toss the fried chicken pieces with the orange sauce until well coated.

5. **Serve:** Place the orange chicken over a bed of cooked white rice. Garnish with chopped green onions and sesame seeds.

6. **Enjoy:** Serve immediately, and savor the delicious homemade Panda Express Orange Chicken!

Nutrition Facts (per serving):

- Calories: 480
- Total Fat: 18g
- Saturated Fat: 3g
- Cholesterol: 180mg
- Sodium: 1200mg
- Total Carbohydrates: 48g
- Dietary Fiber: 1g
- Sugars: 32g
- Protein: 30g

OUTBACK STEAKHOUSE INSPIRED ALICE SPRINGS CHICKEN

Cooking Time: 30 minutes

Servings: 4

Ingredients:

- 4 boneless, skinless chicken breasts
- Salt and pepper to taste
- 1/2 cup Dijon mustard
- 1/2 cup honey
- 2 tablespoons mayonnaise
- 1 teaspoon vegetable oil
- 1 teaspoon garlic powder
- 1 teaspoon onion powder
- 8 slices of cooked bacon
- 1 cup sliced mushrooms
- 2 cups shredded Colby-Jack cheese
- 2 tablespoons chopped fresh parsley (for garnish)

Steps:

1. Preheat your oven to 375°F (190°C).
2. Season the chicken breasts with salt and pepper.
3. Mix Dijon mustard, honey, mayonnaise, garlic powder, and onion powder in a small bowl. Set aside.

4. Heat vegetable oil in an oven-safe skillet over medium-high heat. Sear the seasoned chicken breasts until golden brown on both sides.

5. Remove the chicken from the skillet and set aside. In the same skillet, sauté sliced mushrooms until they are tender.

6. Spread a generous amount of the honey mustard sauce over each chicken breast.

7. Place two slices of cooked bacon on each chicken breast, covering the honey mustard sauce.

8. Spoon the sautéed mushrooms over the bacon.

9. Sprinkle shredded Colby-Jack cheese over the chicken breasts.

10. Transfer the skillet to the preheated oven and bake for 20 minutes or until the chicken is cooked and the cheese is melted and bubbly.

11. Garnish with chopped fresh parsley before serving.

Nutrition Facts: *(Per Serving)*

- Calories: 560
- Total Fat: 28g
  - Saturated Fat: 12g
  - Trans Fat: 0g
- Cholesterol: 145mg
- Sodium: 980mg
- Total Carbohydrates: 32g
  - Dietary Fiber: 1g

- Sugars: 28g
- Protein: 42g

CHICK-FIL-A COBB SALAD REPRODUCTION

Cooking Time: 20 minutes

Serving: 4

Ingredients:

- 2 boneless, skinless chicken breasts
- 1 tablespoon olive oil
- Salt and pepper to taste
- 8 cups mixed salad greens
- 1 cup cherry tomatoes, halved
- 1 cup cucumber, diced
- 1 cup shredded cheddar cheese
- 4 hard-boiled eggs, sliced
- 1 cup crispy bacon, crumbled
- 1 avocado, diced
- 1/2 cup ranch dressing

Steps:

1. **Prepare the Chicken:** Season chicken breasts with salt and pepper. In a skillet over medium-high heat, heat olive oil. Cook chicken breasts for 6-8 minutes per side or until fully cooked. Let them rest for a few minutes, then slice into thin strips.

2. **Assemble the Salad:** In a large bowl, combine the salad greens, cherry tomatoes, cucumber, cheddar cheese, sliced hard-boiled eggs, crispy bacon, and diced avocado.

3. **Add Chicken Strips:** Arrange the sliced chicken on top of the salad.

4. **Drizzle with Dressing:** Pour the ranch dressing over the salad.

5. **Toss Gently:** Toss the salad gently using salad tongs until all ingredients are well combined and evenly coated with the dressing.

6. **Serve:** Divide the salad among four plates.

Nutrition Facts (per serving):

- Calories: 480
- Total Fat: 32g
    - Saturated Fat: 10g
    - Trans Fat: 0g
- Cholesterol: 230mg
- Sodium: 720mg
- Total Carbohydrates: 15g
    - Dietary Fiber: 7g
    - Sugars: 4g
- Protein: 35g

COPYCAT NOODLES & COMPANY PESTO CAVATAPPI

Cooking Time: 20 minutes

 Servings: 4

Ingredients:

- 1 lb cavatappi pasta
- 2 cups fresh basil leaves, packed
- 1/2 cup grated Parmesan cheese
- 1/2 cup pine nuts
- 3 garlic cloves, minced
- 1 cup extra-virgin olive oil
- Salt and pepper to taste
- 1 cup cherry tomatoes, halved
- 1/2 cup black olives, sliced
- 1/4 cup grated Pecorino Romano cheese
- 1/4 cup sun-dried tomatoes, chopped
- Optional: Grilled chicken or shrimp for protein

Steps:

1. **Cook Cavatappi:** Cook the Cavatappi pasta according to package instructions. Drain and set aside.

2. **Prepare Pesto Sauce:** In a food processor, combine basil, Parmesan cheese, pine nuts, and minced garlic. Pulse until finely chopped. With the processor running, slowly pour the olive oil until the mixture forms a smooth sauce. Season with salt and pepper to taste.

3. **Combine Pasta and Pesto:** In a large mixing bowl, toss the cooked cavatappi with the prepared pesto sauce until the pasta is well coated.

4. **Add Toppings:** Gently fold the cherry tomatoes, black olives, and sun-dried tomatoes. If desired, add grilled chicken or shrimp for extra protein.

5. **Serve:** Divide the pesto cavatappi among serving plates. Sprinkle each portion with grated Pecorino Romano cheese.

6. **Optional Garnish:** Garnish with additional fresh basil leaves and a drizzle of olive oil for added flavor.

Nutrition Facts (per serving): *(Note: Nutrition facts may vary based on specific ingredients and optional additions.)*

- Calories: 600
- Protein: 15g
- Fat: 45g
- Carbohydrates: 40g
- Fiber: 5g
- Sugar: 3g
- Sodium: 400mg

INSPIRED BY SHAKE SHACK CHICKEN SHACK

Cooking Time: 30 minutes
Servings: 4

Ingredients:

- 4 boneless, skinless chicken breasts
- 1 cup buttermilk
- 1 cup all-purpose flour
- 1 teaspoon paprika
- 1 teaspoon garlic powder
- 1 teaspoon onion powder
- Salt and pepper to taste
- Vegetable oil for frying

For the Shack Sauce:

- 1/2 cup mayonnaise
- 1 tablespoon ketchup
- 1 tablespoon yellow mustard
- 4 slices of green leaf lettuce
- 4 potato hamburger buns

Steps:

1. **Marinate the Chicken:**
   - Place chicken breasts in a bowl and cover with buttermilk. Let it marinate for at least 15 minutes or overnight for extra flavor.

2. **Prepare the Shack Sauce:**
   - In a small bowl, mix mayonnaise, ketchup, and mustard. Set aside.

3. **Coat the Chicken:**
   - Combine flour, paprika, garlic powder, onion powder, salt, and pepper in a separate

bowl. Remove each chicken breast from the buttermilk, letting excess drip off, and coat in the flour mixture.

4. **Fry the Chicken:**

   - Heat vegetable oil in a large skillet over medium-high heat. Fry the coated chicken breasts for about 4-5 minutes per side or until golden brown and cooked through. Ensure the internal temperature reaches 165°F (74°C).

5. **Assemble the Chicken Shack:**

   - Toast the hamburger buns. Spread Shack Sauce on both sides of the bun.
   - Place a fried chicken breast on the bottom bun.
   - Top with a slice of green leaf lettuce.
   - Place the top bun on the lettuce to complete the sandwich.

6. **Serve:**

   - Serve the Inspired Shake Shack Chicken Shack immediately, pairing it with your favorite sides.

Nutrition Facts:

- **Calories:** 450 per serving
- **Protein:** 28g
- **Fat:** 20g
- **Carbohydrates:** 38g

- **Fiber:** 2g
- **Sugar:** 5g
- **Sodium:** 800mg

TACO BELL CRUNCH WRAP SUPREME AT HOME

Ingredients:

- 1 lb ground beef
- 1 packet of taco seasoning
- 1 cup nacho cheese sauce
- 1 cup sour cream
- 1 cup diced tomatoes
- 1 cup shredded lettuce
- 1 cup shredded cheddar cheese
- 6 large flour tortillas
- 6 tostada shells
- 6 (12-inch) squares of parchment paper

Cooking Time: Approximately 30 minutes

Serving: 6 Crunchwraps

Steps:

1. In a skillet over medium heat, cook the ground beef until browned. Drain excess fat.
2. Add the taco seasoning to the beef according to the packet instructions. Stir well and let it simmer for a few minutes.

3. Heat the nacho cheese sauce in a separate saucepan over low heat.

4. Lay out the flour tortillas on a clean surface. In the center of each tortilla, layer the following ingredients: a spoonful of seasoned ground beef, a tostada shell, a drizzle of nacho cheese sauce, a dollop of sour cream, diced tomatoes, shredded lettuce, and shredded cheddar cheese.

5. Carefully fold the edges of the tortilla up and over the filling, creating a hexagonal shape. Make sure all edges are sealed.

6. Place each wrapped Crunchwrap, seam-side down, on a square of parchment paper.

7. In a clean skillet over medium heat, place the Crunchwraps seam-side down and cook until the bottom is golden brown. Flip and cook the other side until golden brown and the cheese is melted.

8. Remove from heat and let them cool for a minute before serving.

Nutrition Facts (per serving):

- Calories: 550
- Total Fat: 32g
    - Saturated Fat: 15g
    - Trans Fat: 1g
- Cholesterol: 80mg
- Sodium: 1100mg
- Total Carbohydrates: 40g
    - Dietary Fiber: 3g

- Sugars: 3g
- Protein: 25g

HOMEMADE OLIVE GARDEN MINESTRONE SOUP

Cooking Time: 1 hour 30 minutes

Serving: 6

Ingredients:

- 2 tablespoons olive oil
- 1 onion, diced
- 2 carrots, sliced
- 2 celery stalks, chopped
- 3 cloves garlic, minced
- 1 zucchini, diced
- 1 cup green beans, cut into 1-inch pieces
- 1 can (14 oz) diced tomatoes
- 1 can (14 oz) kidney beans, drained and rinsed
- 1 can (14 oz) cannellini beans, drained and rinsed
- 6 cups vegetable broth
- 1 teaspoon dried oregano
- 1 teaspoon dried basil
- 1/2 teaspoon dried thyme
- Salt and pepper to taste
- 1 cup small pasta (such as ditalini)
- 2 cups fresh spinach, chopped

- Grated Parmesan cheese for serving

Steps:

1. In a large pot, heat olive oil over medium heat. Add diced onion, carrots, celery, and garlic. Sauté until the vegetables are tender, about 5-7 minutes.

2. Add zucchini, green beans, diced tomatoes, kidney beans, cannellini beans, vegetable broth, oregano, basil, thyme, salt, and pepper. Bring the soup to a boil, reduce the heat to low, cover, and simmer for 30 minutes.

3. Stir in the pasta and continue to simmer until the pasta is cooked al dente, according to package instructions.

4. Add chopped spinach and cook for 2-3 minutes until the spinach wilts.

5. Adjust the seasoning if needed. Remove the pot from heat.

Nutrition Facts (per serving):

- Calories: 250
- Total Fat: 6g
- Saturated Fat: 1g
- Cholesterol: 0mg
- Sodium: 800mg
- Total Carbohydrates: 40g
- Dietary Fiber: 9g
- Sugars: 6g
- Protein: 10g

RED LOBSTER'S LOBSTER BISQUE REMAKE

Cooking Time: Approximately 1 hour

Serving: 4

Ingredients:

- 2 lobsters, about 1.5 pounds each
- 1/2 cup unsalted butter
- 1/2 cup all-purpose flour
- 1 cup onion, finely chopped
- 1/2 cup celery, finely chopped
- 1/2 cup carrot, finely chopped
- 4 cloves garlic, minced
- 2 tablespoons tomato paste
- 1 teaspoon paprika
- 1/2 teaspoon dried thyme
- 4 cups seafood stock
- 1 cup dry white wine
- 2 cups heavy cream
- Salt and pepper to taste
- Chives for garnish

Steps:

1. **Prepare Lobsters:** Boil the lobsters in a large pot of salted water for about 8-10 minutes. Remove the meat from the shells, reserving the shells for

the stock. Chop the lobster meat into bite-sized pieces.

2. **Make Lobster Stock:** In a large pot, melt 1/4 cup of butter over medium heat. Add the lobster shells and cook until they turn red. Add onion, celery, carrot, and garlic. Cook until vegetables are softened. Stir in tomato paste, paprika, and thyme. Pour in seafood stock and white wine. Simmer for 30 minutes, then strain the stock, discarding solids.

3. **Prepare Roux:** In a separate pot, melt the remaining 1/4 cup of butter over medium heat. Stir in flour to create a roux. Cook, stirring constantly, until the roux turns golden brown.

4. **Combine Ingredients:** Slowly whisk the lobster stock into the roux, ensuring a smooth consistency. Bring the mixture to a simmer. Add the chopped lobster meat and heavy cream. Season with salt and pepper to taste.

5. **Simmer and Serve:** Allow the bisque to simmer for 15-20 minutes, allowing flavors to meld. Ladle the bisque into bowls and garnish with chopped chives.

Nutrition Facts (per serving):

- Calories: 480
- Total Fat: 38g
- Saturated Fat: 23g
- Cholesterol: 210mg
- Sodium: 820mg

- Total Carbohydrates: 15g
- Dietary Fiber: 2g
- Sugars: 4g
- Protein: 18g

CHIPOTLE BARBACOA BURRITO COPYCAT

Cooking Time: 4 hours (includes marination time)
Serving: 4
Ingredients:

- 2 lbs beef chuck roast, cut into large chunks
- 2 chipotle peppers in adobo sauce, minced
- 4 cloves garlic, minced
- 1 small red onion, finely chopped
- 1 tablespoon ground cumin
- 1 tablespoon dried oregano
- 1 teaspoon ground cloves
- 1 teaspoon ground cinnamon
- 1 cup beef broth
- Salt and pepper to taste
- 4 large flour tortillas
- 1 cup cooked white rice
- 1 cup black beans, drained and rinsed
- 1 cup shredded Monterey Jack cheese
- 1 cup guacamole

- 1/2 cup sour cream
- Fresh cilantro, chopped (for garnish)
- Lime wedges (for serving)

Steps:

1. **Marinate the Beef:** In a blender, combine chipotle peppers, garlic, red onion, cumin, oregano, cloves, cinnamon, salt, and pepper. Blend until it forms a smooth paste. Rub the paste all over the beef chunks. Place the beef in a bowl, cover it, and refrigerate it for at least 2 hours or overnight for best results.

2. **Slow Cook the Barbacoa:** Place the marinated beef in a slow cooker. Add beef broth. Cook on low for 7-8 hours or high for 4-5 hours until the beef is tender and easily shreds with a fork.

3. **Shred the Barbacoa:** Once cooked, shred the beef using two forks. Mix the shredded beef with the cooking juices to enhance the flavor.

4. **Assemble the Burritos:** Warm the flour tortillas. On each tortilla, layer a portion of shredded beef, cooked rice, black beans, Monterey Jack cheese, guacamole, and a dollop of sour cream.

5. **Roll the Burritos:** Fold in the sides of the tortilla and then fold up the bottom, tucking it tightly. Roll the burrito from the bottom up, creating a secure wrap.

6. **Serve:** Place the burritos seam-side down on a serving plate. Garnish with chopped cilantro and serve with lime wedges on the side.

Nutrition Facts (per serving):

- Calories: 650
- Total Fat: 32g
  - Saturated Fat: 15g
- Cholesterol: 120mg
- Sodium: 800mg
- Total Carbohydrates: 50g
  - Dietary Fiber: 8g
  - Sugars: 3g
- Protein: 40g

OUTBACK STEAKHOUSE BLOOMIN' ONION

Cooking Time: 20 minutes
Serving: 4
Ingredients:

- 1 large sweet onion
- 2 cups all-purpose flour
- 2 cups buttermilk
- 1 1/2 cups breadcrumbs
- 1 teaspoon paprika
- 1 teaspoon garlic powder
- 1/2 teaspoon cayenne pepper
- Salt and pepper to taste
- Vegetable oil for frying

Steps:

1. **Preparation:** Cut off the onion's top (about 1 inch) and peel. Cut about 1/2 inch off the bottom so it can stand upright. Make 4 vertical cuts, but don't cut all the way through. Turn the onion and make 8-12 cuts horizontally, again not cutting through the onion.

2. **Soaking:** In a bowl, mix the buttermilk, paprika, garlic powder, cayenne pepper, salt, and pepper. Soak the onion in the buttermilk mixture for at least 1 hour.

3. **Coating:** In a separate bowl, mix the flour and breadcrumbs. After the onion has soaked, carefully dredge it in the flour mixture, making sure to get the coating between the layers.

4. **Shaping:** Tap off the excess flour mixture and reshape the onion if needed. Let it rest for 10 minutes to set the coating.

5. **Frying:** Heat the vegetable oil in a deep fryer or a large pot to 375°F (190°C). Carefully lower the coated onion into the hot oil, and fry for about 10 minutes or until golden brown and crispy.

6. **Draining:** Remove the onion from the oil and drain it on paper towels.

7. **Serving:** Serve the Bloomin' Onion with your favorite dipping sauce on a plate.

Nutrition Facts: (PER SERVING)

- Calories: 450
- Total Fat: 15g
  - Saturated Fat: 2g
  - Trans Fat: 0g
- Cholesterol: 5mg
- Sodium: 800mg
- Total Carbohydrates: 70g

- Dietary Fiber: 5g
- Sugars: 8g
- Protein: 12g

COPYCAT OLIVE GARDEN CHICKEN ALFREDO

Cooking Time: 25 minutes
Servings: 4
Ingredients:

- 1 lb fettuccine pasta
- 2 boneless, skinless chicken breasts, thinly sliced
- Salt and black pepper to taste
- 2 tbsp olive oil
- 4 cloves garlic, minced
- 1 cup heavy cream
- 1 cup grated Parmesan cheese
- 1/2 cup unsalted butter
- 1 cup chicken broth
- 1 cup shredded mozzarella cheese
- Fresh parsley, chopped (for garnish)

Steps:

1. **Cook Pasta:** Cook the fettuccine pasta according to package instructions. Drain and set aside.

2. **Season Chicken:** Season the sliced chicken breasts with salt and black pepper.

3. **Sauté Chicken:** Heat olive oil over medium-high heat in a large skillet. Add the sliced chicken and cook until browned and cooked through. Remove chicken from the skillet and set aside.

4. **Prepare Sauce:** In the same skillet, add minced garlic and cook for about 1 minute until fragrant. Add butter, heavy cream, and chicken broth. Stir well and bring to a simmer.

5. **Add Cheese:** Gradually whisk the Parmesan cheese until the sauce is smooth. Reduce heat to low and stir in mozzarella cheese until melted and the sauce is creamy.

6. **Combine Ingredients:** Add the cooked chicken to the sauce and combine. Allow it to simmer for a few minutes until the chicken is heated through.

7. **Combine with Pasta:** Add the cooked fettuccine pasta to the skillet, tossing to coat the pasta evenly with the sauce.

8. **Serve:** Garnish with chopped fresh parsley and additional Parmesan cheese if desired. Serve hot.

Nutrition Facts (per serving):

- Calories: 850
- Total Fat: 48g
  - Saturated Fat: 27g
  - Trans Fat: 1g
- Cholesterol: 220mg
- Sodium: 850mg

- Total Carbohydrates: 60g
  - Dietary Fiber: 3g
  - Sugars: 3g
- Protein: 42g

DIY CHILI'S BABY BACK RIBS

Cooking Time: 3 hours
Serving: 4
Ingredients:

- 2 racks of baby back ribs
- 1 cup of brown sugar
- 1 tablespoon of chili powder
- 1 tablespoon of paprika
- 1 tablespoon of garlic powder
- 1 tablespoon of onion powder
- 1 teaspoon of cayenne pepper
- Salt and black pepper to taste
- 2 cups of your favorite barbecue sauce

Steps:

1. **Preheat the Oven:** Preheat your oven to 275°F (135°C).

2. **Prepare the Ribs:** Remove the membrane from the back of the ribs. Mix brown sugar, chili powder, paprika, garlic powder, onion powder, cayenne pepper, salt, and black pepper in a bowl

to create the rub. Rub the mixture all over the ribs, ensuring they are evenly coated.

3. **Wrap in Foil:** Wrap each rack of ribs tightly in aluminum foil, sealing them well. Place them on a baking sheet.

4. **Bake:** Bake the ribs in the oven for 2.5 to 3 hours or until the meat is tender and easily pulls away from the bone.

5. **Prepare the Grill:** Preheat your grill to medium-high heat.

6. **Finish on the Grill:** Remove the ribs from the foil and brush them generously with your favorite barbecue sauce. Grill the ribs for 10-15 minutes, turning occasionally and basting with more barbecue sauce until they develop a nice caramelized crust.

7. **Serve:** Once done, let the ribs rest for a few minutes before slicing. Serve with extra barbecue sauce on the side.

Nutrition Facts: (PER SERVING)

- Calories: 600
- Total Fat: 40g
- Saturated Fat: 15g
- Cholesterol: 150mg
- Sodium: 1200mg
- Total Carbohydrates: 30g
- Dietary Fiber: 1g

- Sugars: 25g

- Protein: 30g

INSPIRED PF CHANG'S ORANGE CHICKEN

Cooking Time: 30 minutes
Serving: 4
Ingredients:

- 1 lb boneless, skinless chicken thighs cut into bite-sized pieces

- 1 cup cornstarch

- 2 eggs, beaten

- 1/4 cup vegetable oil

FOR THE SAUCE:

- 1/2 cup orange juice

- 1/4 cup soy sauce

- 1/4 cup rice vinegar

- 3 tablespoons honey

- 2 cloves garlic, minced

- 1 teaspoon ginger, grated

- 1 tablespoon cornstarch mixed with 2 tablespoons water (for thickening)

FOR GARNISH:

- Sesame seeds

- Green onions, chopped

Steps:

1. **Coat the Chicken:** Coat the chicken pieces in a bowl with cornstarch, shaking off excess. Dip each piece into beaten eggs.

2. **Fry the Chicken:** Heat vegetable oil in a large skillet over medium-high heat. Fry the chicken until golden brown and cooked through. Remove and set aside.

3. **Make the Sauce:** In the same skillet, combine orange juice, soy sauce, rice vinegar, honey, minced garlic, and grated ginger. Bring to a simmer.

4. **Thicken the Sauce:** Mix 1 tablespoon of cornstarch with 2 tablespoons of water in a small bowl. Stir the mixture into the sauce and cook until it thickens.

5. **Combine Chicken and Sauce:** Add the fried chicken to the sauce, tossing to coat evenly.

6. **Garnish and Serve:** Sprinkle sesame seeds and chopped green onions over the orange chicken. Serve over steamed rice.

Nutrition Facts (per serving):

- Calories: 450
- Total Fat: 16g
- Saturated Fat: 3g
- Cholesterol: 150mg
- Sodium: 800mg
- Total Carbohydrates: 45g

- Dietary Fiber: 1g
- Sugars: 18g
- Protein: 30g

TEXAS ROADHOUSE COPYCAT ROLLS WITH CINNAMON BUTTER

Cooking Time: 2 hours (including rising time)
Serving: 12 rolls
Ingredients:
For the Rolls:

- 1 cup warm milk (110°F/43°C)
- 2 tablespoons active dry yeast
- 1/4 cup granulated sugar
- 4 cups all-purpose flour
- 1/4 cup unsalted butter, melted
- 1 large egg
- 1 teaspoon salt

For the Cinnamon Butter:

- 1/2 cup unsalted butter, softened
- 1/4 cup powdered sugar
- 1 teaspoon ground cinnamon
- 1/4 teaspoon vanilla extract

Steps:

1. In a small bowl, combine warm milk, yeast, and sugar. Let it sit for 5-10 minutes until it becomes frothy.

2. In a large mixing bowl, combine 3 1/2 cups of flour, melted butter, egg, salt, and the yeast mixture. Mix until a dough forms.

3. Knead the dough on a floured surface for about 5-7 minutes, incorporating the remaining 1/2 cup of flour until the dough is smooth and elastic.

4. Place the dough in a greased bowl, cover it with a damp cloth, and let it rise in a warm place for 1 hour or until it doubles in size.

5. Preheat the oven to 350°F (175°C). Punch down the dough and divide it into 12 equal portions. Roll each portion into a ball and place in a greased baking dish.

6. Cover the rolls and let them rise for an additional 30 minutes.

7. Bake the rolls for 15-20 minutes or until they turn golden brown.

8. While the rolls are baking, prepare the cinnamon butter by combining softened butter, powdered sugar, cinnamon, and vanilla extract. Mix until well combined.

9. Once the rolls are done, brush them with melted butter and serve with the cinnamon butter.

Nutrition Facts (per serving):

- Calories: 280
- Total Fat: 12g
    - Saturated Fat: 7g
    - Trans Fat: 0g

- Cholesterol: 45mg
- Sodium: 200mg
- Total Carbohydrates: 36g
    - Dietary Fiber: 2g
    - Sugars: 8g
- Protein: 5g

CRISPY COPYCAT KFC FRIED CHICKEN

Cooking Time: 40 minutes
Serving: 4
Ingredients:

- 8 pieces of chicken (mix of drumsticks and thighs)
- 2 cups buttermilk
- 2 cups all-purpose flour
- 2 teaspoons paprika
- 1 teaspoon dried thyme
- 1 teaspoon garlic powder
- 1 teaspoon onion powder
- 1 teaspoon salt
- 1 teaspoon black pepper
- 1/2 teaspoon cayenne pepper
- Vegetable oil for frying

Steps:

1. **Marinate the Chicken:**
    - Place the chicken pieces in a large bowl.

- Pour buttermilk over the chicken, ensuring each piece is well-coated.
- Cover and refrigerate for at least 2 hours or overnight for best results.

1. **Prepare the Coating:**
   - Combine flour, paprika, thyme, garlic powder, onion powder, salt, black pepper, and cayenne pepper in a shallow dish. Mix well.

1. **Coat the Chicken:**
   - Preheat the vegetable oil in a deep fryer or deep skillet to 350°F (175°C).
   - Remove chicken from the buttermilk, allowing excess to drip off.
   - Coat each piece with the seasoned flour mixture, pressing the coating onto the chicken.

1. **Fry the Chicken:**
   - Carefully place the coated chicken pieces into the hot oil.
   - Fry for about 15-20 minutes, turning occasionally, until the chicken is golden brown and cooked through (internal temperature should reach 165°F or 74°C).

1. **Drain and Serve:**
   - Remove the fried chicken from the oil and place it on a wire rack or paper towel to drain any excess oil.
   - Allow it to rest for a few minutes before serving.

Nutrition Facts (per serving):

- Calories: 450
- Total Fat: 25g
  - Saturated Fat: 6g
  - Trans Fat: 0g
- Cholesterol: 120mg
- Sodium: 800mg
- Total Carbohydrates: 22g
  - Dietary Fiber: 1g
  - Sugars: 2g
- Protein: 32g

HOMEMADE APPLEBEE'S BOURBON STREET CHICKEN

Cooking Time: 30 minutes
Servings: 4
Ingredients:

- 4 boneless, skinless chicken breasts
- 1 cup soy sauce
- 1 cup brown sugar
- 1/4 cup bourbon
- 2 cloves garlic, minced
- 1 teaspoon ground ginger
- 1/2 teaspoon black pepper
- 1 tablespoon vegetable oil
- 2 green onions, sliced (for garnish)

- Sesame seeds (for garnish)

Steps:

1. Combine soy sauce, brown sugar, bourbon, minced garlic, ground ginger, and black pepper in a bowl. Stir until the sugar is dissolved.

2. Place chicken breasts in a large resealable plastic bag and pour half of the marinade over them. Seal the bag and refrigerate for at least 1 hour (or overnight for more flavor).

3. Heat vegetable oil in a large skillet over medium-high heat.

4. Remove chicken from the marinade and discard the marinade from the bag.

5. Cook the chicken in the skillet for 6-8 minutes per side or until cooked through and no longer pink in the center.

6. In the last few minutes of cooking, pour the remaining marinade over the chicken and allow it to simmer and thicken.

7. Once the chicken is cooked, transfer it to a serving platter, pouring the thickened sauce over the top.

8. Garnish with sliced green onions and sprinkle with sesame seeds.

9. Serve the Bourbon Street Chicken over rice or with your favorite side dishes.

Nutrition Facts (per serving):

- Calories: 350
- Total Fat: 8g
- Saturated Fat: 2g
- Cholesterol: 90mg
- Sodium: 1200mg
- Total Carbohydrates: 30g
- Dietary Fiber: 1g
- Sugars: 26g
- Protein: 30g

PAN-SEARED RED LOBSTER-STYLE LOBSTER TAILS

Cooking Time: 15 minutes
Serving: 2
Ingredients:

- 2 lobster tails (6-8 ounces each)
- 2 tablespoons olive oil
- 2 cloves garlic, minced
- 2 tablespoons fresh parsley, chopped
- Salt and pepper to taste
- Lemon wedges for serving

Steps:

1. **Prepare the Lobster Tails:**
   - Thaw the frozen lobster tails and pat them dry with paper towels.

- Use kitchen shears to cut through the top of the shell, stopping at the tail.
- Gently lift the lobster meat from the shell, keeping it attached at the base. Place the meat on top of the shell.

1. **Season the Lobster Tails:**
   - Season the lobster tails with salt and pepper on both sides.

1. **Sear the Lobster Tails:**
   - Heat olive oil in a skillet over medium-high heat.
   - Add minced garlic to the pan and sauté for 30 seconds until fragrant.
   - Place the lobster tails in the skillet, meat side down, and sear for 4-5 minutes until the meat is golden brown.

1. **Flip and Cook:**
   - Carefully flip the lobster tails using tongs.
   - Continue to cook for 4-5 minutes, basting the meat with the garlic-infused oil.

1. **Garnish and Serve:**
   - Sprinkle chopped parsley over the lobster tails during the last minute of cooking.
   - Transfer the lobster tails to a serving plate and drizzle with any remaining pan juices.
   - Serve hot with lemon wedges on the side.

Nutrition Facts (per serving):

- Calories: 250
- Protein: 20g

- Fat: 15g
- Carbohydrates: 2g
- Fiber: 0.5g
- Sugars: 0g
- Cholesterol: 90mg
- Sodium: 350mg

COPYCAT TGI FRIDAY'S JACK DANIEL'S GLAZED CHICKEN

Cooking Time: 45 minutes
Serving: 4
Ingredients:

- 4 boneless, skinless chicken breasts
- Salt and pepper to taste
- 1 cup flour
- 2 tablespoons olive oil

For the Jack Daniel's Glaze:

- 1 cup Jack Daniel's Tennessee Whiskey
- 1 cup brown sugar
- 1/2 cup soy sauce
- 1/4 cup Dijon mustard
- 2 cloves garlic, minced
- 1 teaspoon ginger, grated

For Garnish:

- Sesame seeds

- Chopped green onions

Steps:

1. Season the chicken breasts with salt and pepper. Coat them with flour, shaking off any excess.

2. Heat olive oil in a large skillet over medium-high heat. Cook the chicken breasts until golden brown on both sides and cooked through. Remove from the skillet and set aside.

3. Combine Jack Daniel's, brown sugar, soy sauce, Dijon mustard, minced garlic, and grated ginger in the same skillet. Bring to a simmer and cook for 15-20 minutes or until the sauce thickens.

4. Return the cooked chicken to the skillet, turning to coat each piece with the glaze. Allow it to simmer for 5-10 minutes until the chicken absorbs the flavors.

5. Sprinkle sesame seeds and chopped green onions on top for garnish.

Nutrition Facts (per serving):

- Calories: 450
- Total Fat: 12g
- Saturated Fat: 2g
- Cholesterol: 100mg
- Sodium: 1200mg
- Total Carbohydrates: 40g
- Dietary Fiber: 1g

- Sugars: 30g
- Protein: 30g

CHEESECAKE FACTORY'S BANG CHICKEN AND SHRIMP

Cooking Time: 30 minutes
Servings: 4
Ingredients:

- 1 pound chicken breast, thinly sliced
- 1/2 pound large shrimp, peeled and deveined
- 1 cup buttermilk
- 1 cup all-purpose flour
- 1 cup panko breadcrumbs
- Salt and pepper to taste
- 1 cup Bang Bang Sauce (recipe below)
- 1/4 cup chopped green onions, for garnish
- Cooked rice for serving

Bang Bang Sauce:

- 1/2 cup mayonnaise
- 1/4 cup sweet chili sauce
- 1 tablespoon honey
- 1 tablespoon Sriracha sauce
- 1 teaspoon soy sauce

Steps:

1. **Marinate the Chicken and Shrimp:**

- In separate bowls, marinate the chicken slices in buttermilk and the shrimp in buttermilk for about 15-20 minutes.
- Season the chicken with salt and pepper.

1. **Prepare the Breading Stations:**
   - Place the flour, panko breadcrumbs, and a mixture of equal parts flour and breadcrumbs in three separate shallow bowls.
   - Take each piece of chicken and shrimp from the buttermilk, allowing excess liquid to drip off.

1. **Bread the Chicken and Shrimp:**
   - Dredge the chicken in flour, then dip into the flour and breadcrumb mixture, pressing the breadcrumbs onto the chicken.
   - Repeat the process for the shrimp.
   - Ensure each piece is evenly coated.

1. **Fry the Chicken and Shrimp:**
   - Heat oil in a deep skillet or fryer to 350°F (175°C).
   - Fry the chicken and shrimp in batches until golden brown and cooked through, about 3-4 minutes for the chicken and 2-3 minutes for the shrimp.
   - Place on a paper towel-lined plate to drain excess oil.

1. **Make the Bang Bang Sauce:**
   - Whisk together mayonnaise, sweet chili sauce, honey, Sriracha, and soy sauce in a bowl until well combined.

1. **Coat the Chicken and Shrimp:**
   - Toss the fried chicken and shrimp in the prepared Bang Bang Sauce until well coated.

1. **Serve:**
   - Serve the Bang Chicken and Shrimp over cooked rice.
   - Garnish with chopped green onions.

Nutrition Facts (per serving):

- Calories: 550
- Protein: 35g
- Carbohydrates: 45g
- Fat: 25g
- Fiber: 2g
- Sugar: 12g
- Sodium: 1200mg

CHEESECAKE FACTORY'S LOUISIANA CHICKEN PASTA

Cooking Time: 30 minutes
Serving: 4
Ingredients:

- 8 oz linguine pasta
- 2 boneless, skinless chicken breasts, thinly sliced
- Cajun seasoning (to taste)
- 2 tbsp olive oil

- 1 red bell pepper, thinly sliced
- 1 yellow bell pepper, thinly sliced
- 1 green bell pepper, thinly sliced
- 1 small red onion, thinly sliced
- 3 cloves garlic, minced
- 1 cup cherry tomatoes, halved
- 1 cup heavy cream
- 1/2 cup chicken broth
- 1/2 cup Parmesan cheese, grated
- Salt and black pepper (to taste)
- Fresh parsley, chopped (for garnish)

Steps:

1. Cook linguine pasta according to package instructions. Drain and set aside.

2. Season chicken breasts with Cajun seasoning on both sides.

3. In a large skillet, heat olive oil over medium-high heat. Add seasoned chicken and cook until browned and cooked through. Remove from the skillet and set aside.

4. In the same skillet, add a bit more olive oil if needed. Sauté red, yellow, and green bell peppers, red onion, and minced garlic until vegetables are tender.

5. Add cherry tomatoes to the skillet and cook for 2-3 minutes.

6. Pour in the heavy cream and chicken broth. Bring to a simmer.

7. Stir in Parmesan cheese until the sauce thickens. Season with salt and black pepper to taste.

8. Add the cooked chicken back to the skillet, allowing it to heat through.

9. Toss the cooked linguine in the skillet, ensuring it is well coated with the sauce and ingredients.

10. Serve the Louisiana Chicken Pasta on individual plates, garnished with chopped fresh parsley.

Nutrition Facts:

NOTE: NUTRITIONAL VALUES ARE APPROXIMATE AND MAY VARY BASED ON SPECIFIC INGREDIENTS.

- Calories: 650 per serving
- Total Fat: 28g
- Saturated Fat: 14g
- Cholesterol: 120mg
- Sodium: 550mg
- Total Carbohydrates: 57g
- Dietary Fiber: 4g
- Sugars: 6g
- Protein: 42g

APPLEBEE'S ORIENTAL CHICKEN SALAD RECREATION

Cooking Time: 30 minutes

 Servings: 4

Ingredients:

- 1 pound boneless, skinless chicken breasts
- Salt and pepper to taste
- 1 cup buttermilk
- 1 cup all-purpose flour
- 1 cup Panko breadcrumbs
- 1/2 cup sesame seeds
- 1/4 cup vegetable oil
- 8 cups mixed salad greens
- 1 cup red cabbage, shredded
- 1 cup carrots, julienned
- 1 cup crispy chow mein noodles
- 1 cup mandarin orange segments, drained

For the Dressing:

- 1/4 cup honey
- 3 tablespoons rice vinegar
- 1/4 cup mayonnaise
- 1 tablespoon Dijon mustard
- 1 tablespoon sesame oil
- Salt and pepper to taste

Steps:

1. Preheat the oven to 375°F (190°C).

2. Season the chicken breasts with salt and pepper. Dip each piece into buttermilk, then dredge in flour, Panko breadcrumbs, and sesame seeds.

3. Heat vegetable oil in an oven-safe skillet over medium-high heat. Sear the chicken on both sides until golden brown.

4. Transfer the skillet to the preheated oven and bake for 15-20 minutes or until the chicken is cooked.

5. While the chicken is baking, prepare the dressing in a bowl by whisking together honey, rice vinegar, mayonnaise, Dijon mustard, sesame oil, salt, and pepper.

6. Remove the chicken from the oven and let it rest for a few minutes. Slice it into thin strips.

7. Toss the salad greens, red cabbage, carrots, crispy chow mein noodles, and mandarin orange segments in a large bowl.

8. Divide the salad among four plates, arrange sliced chicken on top, and drizzle with the prepared dressing.

Nutrition Facts (per serving):

- Calories: 520
- Total Fat: 24g
- Saturated Fat: 4g
- Cholesterol: 80mg
- Sodium: 550mg

- Total Carbohydrates: 52g
- Dietary Fiber: 5g
- Sugars: 22g
- Protein: 26g

DIY OLIVE GARDEN SHRIMP SCAMPI

Cooking Time: 20 minutes
 Serving: 4
Ingredients:

- 1 pound large shrimp, peeled and deveined
- 8 ounces linguine or spaghetti
- 4 tablespoons unsalted butter
- 4 tablespoons olive oil
- 4 cloves garlic, minced
- 1/2 teaspoon red pepper flakes (adjust to taste)
- 1/2 cup chicken broth
- 1/4 cup dry white wine
- Salt and black pepper to taste
- 1/4 cup fresh parsley, chopped
- 1 tablespoon lemon juice
- Grated Parmesan cheese for serving

Steps:

1. **Cook the Pasta:** Boil the linguine or spaghetti according to package instructions. Drain and set aside.

2. **Prepare the Shrimp:** Pat the shrimp dry with paper towels. Season with salt and black pepper.

3. **Sauté Shrimp:** Heat 2 tablespoons of butter and 2 tablespoons of olive oil over medium-high heat in a large skillet. Add the shrimp and cook for 1-2 minutes per side until they turn pink. Remove the shrimp from the skillet and set aside.

4. **Prepare the Sauce:** Add the remaining butter and olive oil in the same skillet. Sauté the minced garlic and red pepper flakes until fragrant.

5. **Deglaze the Pan:** Pour in the chicken broth and white wine, scraping any browned bits from the bottom of the pan. Simmer for 2-3 minutes to reduce slightly.

6. **Combine Shrimp and Pasta:** Return the cooked shrimp to the skillet. Add the cooked pasta, tossing to coat in the sauce.

7. **Finish the Dish:** Stir in chopped parsley and lemon juice. Adjust seasoning with salt and black pepper.

8. **Serve:** Divide the shrimp and pasta among plates. Drizzle with extra sauce from the pan. Sprinkle with grated Parmesan cheese.

Nutrition Facts (per serving):

- Calories: 450
- Protein: 25g
- Carbohydrates: 35g

- Fat: 22g
- Saturated Fat: 8g
- Cholesterol: 180mg
- Sodium: 600mg
- Fiber: 2g
- Sugar: 1g

COPYCAT CARRABBA'S CHICKEN BRYAN

Cooking Time: 30 minutes
Serving: 4 servings

INGREDIENTS:

- 4 boneless, skinless chicken breasts
- Salt and pepper to taste
- 2 tablespoons olive oil

FOR THE GOAT CHEESE TOPPING:

- 4 ounces goat cheese, softened
- 2 tablespoons sun-dried tomatoes, chopped
- 2 tablespoons fresh basil, chopped
- 1 tablespoon fresh chives, chopped
- 1 clove garlic, minced

FOR THE LEMON BUTTER SAUCE:

- 1/2 cup unsalted butter
- 1/4 cup white wine
- 2 tablespoons fresh lemon juice

- 1 teaspoon lemon zest
- 1 teaspoon dried oregano
- Salt and pepper to taste

STEPS:

1. Preheat your grill or grill pan over medium-high heat.
2. Season the chicken breasts with salt and pepper, then brush them with olive oil.
3. Grill the chicken breasts for about 6-8 minutes per side or until fully cooked.
4. Mix the goat cheese, sun-dried tomatoes, basil, chives, and minced garlic in a bowl. Set aside.
5. In a small saucepan, melt the butter over medium heat. Add white wine, lemon juice, lemon zest, and dried oregano. Season with salt and pepper. Simmer for 5 minutes, stirring occasionally.
6. Remove the chicken from the grill and place each breast on a serving plate.
7. Spoon a generous amount of goat cheese topping over each chicken breast.
8. Drizzle the lemon butter sauce over the top of the goat cheese.
9. Serve the chicken Bryan hot, garnished with additional fresh basil and chives if desired.

Nutrition Facts (per serving):

- Calories: 480
- Total Fat: 32g
- Saturated Fat: 16g
- Cholesterol: 160mg
- Sodium: 450mg

- Total Carbohydrates: 3g
- Dietary Fiber: 1g
- Sugars: 1g
- Protein: 44g

PANERA BREAD'S BBQ CHICKEN SALAD AT HOME

Cooking Time: 20 minutes
Serving: 4
Ingredients:

- 1 lb boneless, skinless chicken breasts
- Salt and pepper to taste
- 1 tablespoon olive oil
- 1 cup corn kernels (fresh or frozen)
- 1 can (15 oz) black beans, drained and rinsed
- 1 cup cherry tomatoes, halved
- 1/2 red onion, finely chopped
- 1 cup shredded cheddar cheese
- 1/2 cup crispy tortilla strips
- 1/2 cup barbecue sauce
- 1/4 cup ranch dressing
- Fresh cilantro for garnish

Steps:

1. **Season and Cook Chicken:** Season the chicken breasts with salt and pepper. In a large skillet, heat olive oil over medium-high heat. Cook the

chicken breasts until golden brown and cooked through, about 5-7 minutes per side. Brush the cooked chicken with barbecue sauce during the last 2 minutes. Remove from heat and let it rest for a few minutes before slicing.

2. **Prepare Salad Base:** In a large salad bowl, combine corn, black beans, cherry tomatoes, red onion, and shredded cheddar cheese.

3. **Assemble Salad:** Slice the cooked chicken into strips. Add the chicken strips to the salad bowl. Drizzle barbecue sauce and ranch dressing over the salad.

4. **Toss and Serve:** Gently toss all the ingredients until well combined and coated with the dressing.

5. **Top with Crunchy Tortilla Strips:** Sprinkle crispy tortilla strips over the salad for added crunch and texture.

6. **Garnish and Serve:** Garnish the salad with fresh cilantro. Serve immediately, and enjoy the delicious Panera Bread-inspired BBQ Chicken Salad!

Nutrition Facts (per serving):

- Calories: 480
- Total Fat: 20g
  - Saturated Fat: 8g
  - Trans Fat: 0g
- Cholesterol: 100mg

- Sodium: 820mg
- Total Carbohydrates: 38g
  - Dietary Fiber: 8g
  - Sugars: 12g
- Protein: 36g

CHILI'S INSPIRED MOLTEN LAVA CAKE

Cooking Time: 15 minutes
Servings: 4
Ingredients:

- 1 cup semi-sweet chocolate chips
- 1/2 cup unsalted butter
- 1/4 cup all-purpose flour
- 1/2 cup powdered sugar
- 2 large eggs
- 2 egg yolks
- 1 teaspoon vanilla extract
- Pinch of salt
- 4 ramekins (6-ounce size)

Steps:

1. Preheat your oven to 425°F (220°C). Grease the ramekins with butter and dust with a little flour.

2. In a microwave-safe bowl, melt the chocolate chips and butter together in 30-second intervals, stirring until smooth. Allow the mixture to cool slightly.

3. In a separate bowl, sift together the flour and powdered sugar.

4. Whisk the eggs, egg yolks, vanilla extract, and a pinch of salt until well combined.

5. Gradually fold the melted chocolate mixture into the egg mixture until smooth.

6. Add the sifted flour and powdered sugar to the chocolate and egg mixture, folding until combined. Be careful not to overmix.

7. Divide the batter evenly among the prepared ramekins.

8. Place the ramekins on a baking sheet and bake in the oven for 12-14 minutes, or until the edges are set, but the center is still soft.

9. Remove from the oven and let the cakes cool for a minute. Run a knife around the edges of the ramekins to loosen the cakes, then invert each onto a plate.

10. Serve immediately, either on its own or with a scoop of vanilla ice cream.

Nutrition Facts (per serving):

- Calories: 450
- Total Fat: 32g
  - Saturated Fat: 18g
  - Trans Fat: 0g
- Cholesterol: 185mg
- Sodium: 50mg

- Total Carbohydrates: 38g
  - Dietary Fiber: 3g
  - Sugars: 28g
- Protein: 6g

HOMEMADE IN-N-OUT DOUBLE-DOUBLE BURGER

Cooking Time: 20 minutes
Servings: 4 burgers
Ingredients:

- 1 pound ground beef (80% lean)
- 1 pound ground chuck (20% fat)
- Salt and pepper to taste
- 4 hamburger buns
- 4 slices American cheese
- 1 cup iceberg lettuce, shredded
- 1 large tomato, sliced
- 1/2 cup yellow onion, finely diced
- 1/4 cup dill pickles, sliced
- 1/4 cup mayonnaise
- 2 tablespoons ketchup
- 2 tablespoons yellow mustard

Steps:

1. **Preheat the Grill:** Preheat your grill or stovetop griddle to medium-high heat.

2. **Prepare the Patties:** Gently combine the ground beef and chuck in a large bowl. Divide the mixture into 8 equal portions and shape them into thin patties. Season both sides with salt and pepper.

3. **Grill the Patties:** Cook the patties on the preheated grill for 3-4 minutes per side or until they reach your desired level of doneness. Place a slice of American cheese on each patty during the last minute of cooking.

4. **Toast the Buns:** Cut the hamburger buns in half and lightly toast them on the grill for about 1 minute.

5. **Assemble the Burgers:** Spread a tablespoon of mayonnaise on the bottom half of each bun. Place a cheese-covered patty on top, followed by a slice of tomato, shredded lettuce, diced onion, and pickle slices. Top with another patty and the other half of the bun.

6. **Prepare the Sauce:** Mix ketchup and mustard in a small bowl to create the In-N-Out sauce. Spread a dollop of the sauce on the top half of each bun.

7. **Serve:** Your Homemade In-N-Out Double-Double Burgers are ready to be served! Enjoy with your favorite side dishes.

Nutrition Facts (per serving):

- Calories: 650
- Total Fat: 42g
  - Saturated Fat: 18g

- Trans Fat: 1g
- Cholesterol: 120mg
- Sodium: 950mg
- Total Carbohydrates: 30g
  - Dietary Fiber: 2g
  - Sugars: 5g
- Protein: 35g

TEXAS ROADHOUSE RATTLESNAKE BITES COPYCAT

Cooking Time: 20 minutes
Servings: 4
Ingredients:

- 1 cup Monterey Jack cheese, shredded
- 1 cup Colby cheese, shredded
- 1/2 cup diced jalapeños (pickled or fresh, depending on your preference)
- 1/2 cup diced green chilies
- 1/4 cup diced red bell pepper
- 1/4 cup diced green onions
- 2 cups all-purpose flour
- 1 tablespoon baking powder
- 1 teaspoon salt
- 1 cup milk
- Vegetable oil for frying

Steps:

1. In a large bowl, combine the shredded Monterey Jack and Colby cheeses.

2. Add diced jalapeños, green chilies, red bell pepper, and green onions to the cheese mixture. Mix well to combine.

3. Whisk together the flour, baking powder, and salt in a separate bowl.

4. Gradually add the dry ingredients to the cheese mixture, alternating with the milk. Stir until a thick batter forms.

5. Heat vegetable oil in a deep fryer or large pan to 350°F (175°C).

6. Drop rounded portions of the batter into the hot oil using a spoon or cookie scoop. Fry until golden brown, about 3-4 minutes.

7. Remove the bites from the oil and place them on a paper towel-lined plate to drain excess oil.

8. Serve the Rattlesnake Bites hot with your favorite dipping sauce.

Nutrition Facts (per serving):

- Calories: 450
- Total Fat: 25g
  - Saturated Fat: 14g
  - Trans Fat: 0g
- Cholesterol: 60mg
- Sodium: 980mg

- Total Carbohydrates: 42g
  - Dietary Fiber: 2g
  - Sugars: 3g
- Protein: 15g

INSPIRED BY P.F. CHANG'S MONGOLIAN BEEF

Cooking Time: 30 minutes
Serving: 4
Ingredients:

- 1 lb flank steak, thinly sliced
- 1/2 cup cornstarch
- 3 tablespoons vegetable oil
- 2 teaspoons ginger, minced
- 3 cloves garlic, minced
- 1/2 cup low-sodium soy sauce
- 1/2 cup water
- 1/2 cup brown sugar, packed
- 1/2 cup green onions, chopped
- 1/2 teaspoon red pepper flakes (optional)
- Sesame seeds for garnish
- Cooked white or brown rice for serving

Steps:

1. **Coat the Beef:** In a large bowl, toss the thinly sliced flank steak in cornstarch until fully coated.

2. **Heat the Oil:** Heat vegetable oil over medium-high heat in a wok or large skillet.

3. **Cook the Beef:** Add the coated steak to the hot oil, ensuring the pan is not overcrowded. Cook until the Beef is crispy and browned. Remove the Beef and set it aside.

4. **Prepare the Sauce:** In the same pan, add ginger and garlic, sauté for about 1 minute until fragrant. Mix in soy sauce, water, and brown sugar. Stir until the sugar is dissolved.

5. **Combine and Simmer:** Return the cooked Beef to the pan, coating it with the sauce. Add green onions and red pepper flakes (if using). Simmer for an additional 2-3 minutes until the sauce thickens.

6. **Serve:** Garnish with sesame seeds and serve the Mongolian Beef over cooked rice.

Nutrition Facts: (PER SERVING)
Calories: 450
Total Fat: 14g
Saturated Fat: 3g
Cholesterol: 45mg
Sodium: 800mg
Total Carbohydrates: 55g
Dietary Fiber: 2g
Sugars: 28g
Protein: 25g

CRACKER BARREL'S COUNTRY FRIED STEAK DUPLICATION

Cooking Time: 30 minutes
Servings: 4
Ingredients:

- 4 cube steaks
- 1 cup all-purpose flour
- 1 teaspoon salt
- 1/2 teaspoon black pepper
- 1/2 teaspoon garlic powder
- 1/2 teaspoon onion powder
- 1/2 teaspoon paprika
- 1/4 teaspoon cayenne pepper
- 1 cup buttermilk
- Vegetable oil for frying

Steps:

1. **Prepare the Steaks:** Season the cube steaks with salt and pepper on both sides.

2. **Create the Flour Mixture:** In a shallow dish, combine the all-purpose flour, salt, black pepper, garlic powder, onion powder, paprika, and cayenne pepper.

3. **Dip in Buttermilk:** Dip each seasoned cube steak into the buttermilk, making sure to coat it completely.

4. **Coat with Flour Mixture:** Dredge the buttermilk-coated steaks in the flour mixture, pressing the flour onto the steak to ensure a good coating.

5. **Heat Vegetable Oil:** In a large skillet, heat enough vegetable oil to cover the bottom of the pan over medium-high heat.

6. **Fry the Steaks:** Carefully place the coated steaks into the hot oil. Fry each side for about 4-5 minutes or until golden brown and cooked through.

7. **Drain and Rest:** Once cooked, place the country-fried steaks on a paper towel-lined plate to drain excess oil. Allow them to rest for a few minutes.

8. **Serve:** Serve the country-fried steaks hot with your favorite side dishes.

Nutrition Facts: (PER SERVING)

- Calories: 400
- Total Fat: 20g
- Saturated Fat: 6g
- Cholesterol: 80mg
- Sodium: 800mg
- Total Carbohydrates: 30g
- Dietary Fiber: 2g
- Sugars: 3g
- Protein: 25g

CONCLUSION

As you conclude your culinary exploration with the "Copycat Cookbook for Beginners," we hope this journey has sparked newfound excitement and confidence in your kitchen endeavors. By recreating beloved restaurant dishes in the comfort of your home, you've expanded your culinary repertoire and discovered the joy of mastering the art of copycat cooking.

In these pages, you've embarked on a flavorful adventure, from breakfast to dinner, uncovering the secrets behind iconic dishes and putting your spin on restaurant favorites. As you savor the fruits of your labor, whether the aroma of a homemade Olive Garden soup or the satisfaction of crafting a perfect copycat In-N-Out burger, we trust you've experienced the magic that happens when passion meets the stove.

Remember, the world of copycat cooking is ever evolving, with endless possibilities awaiting your creative touch. Use the skills you've acquired here as a foundation to experiment, innovate, and continue bringing the essence of your favorite eateries into your culinary creations.

Whether you're a beginner finding your way around the kitchen or an experienced cook seeking fresh inspiration, we hope this cookbook has empowered you to confidently approach copycat cooking. The joy of sharing restaurant-quality meals with family and friends is now at your fingertips, and we encourage you to keep exploring, experimenting, and delighting in the delicious results.

Thank you for joining us on this delectable journey through the world of copycat cooking. May your kitchen continue to be a space where the love for good food and the joy of creating memorable meals harmonize harmoniously. Happy cooking!

Made in United States
Troutdale, OR
12/02/2024

25598522R00076